Bible plants can be arranged for both beauty
and religious meaning. Here are palm leaves,
papyrus, myrtle, acanthus, lotus lily and leaves,
grapes, apricots, leek and cucumber.

Bible Plants for American Gardens

by

ELEANOR ANTHONY KING

Dover Publications, Inc., New York

Appreciation

My thanks to the staff of the New York Botanical Garden for generous help, especially to Harold N. Moldenke who has shared with me the results of his own work on Bible plants.

Published in Canada by General Publishing Company, Ltd., 30 Lesmill Road, Don Mills, Toronto, Ontario.

Published in the United Kingdom by Constable and Company, Ltd., 10 Orange Street, London WC 2.

This Dover edition, first published in 1975, is an unabridged republication of the work originally published by The Macmillan Company in 1941.

International Standard Book Number: 0-486-23188-7
Library of Congress Catalog Card Number: 75-3646

Manufactured in the United States of America
Dover Publications, Inc.
180 Varick Street
New York, N.Y. 10014

Contents

Illustrations

In Bible days, as now, the fate of nations depended upon wheat fields and the supply of bread.

Introduction

As THIS is written, New Yorkers are crowding to gaze through glass at the Great Chalice of Antioch—which may or may not have been used at the Last Supper; authorities disagree, but the cup inside the reliquary, though of worn and tarnished silver, is beyond price. It must be carefully guarded from the fingers of those who would touch, in reverent ecstasy, a relic which may have been seen and handled by Jesus.

Outside in the spring sunshine, a sidewalk flower-vendor is selling anemones. For a few cents you may hold a handful of ruby and amethyst chalices, glowing like the jeweled Grail of legend. Yet there is no doubt that these are the flowers of the field which Jesus saw and touched, which he used to make his teachings clear to the people.

Plants mentioned in the Bible are the living link between us and the people of those hallowed and distant times. We cultivate in the flower and herb garden, in the vegetable patch and orchard, plants which grew in the gardens of the Promised Land, plants of which Isaiah and Ezekiel spoke, plants which Jesus used in his parables. Today, in America, we grow the almond, the apricot, the fig, the olive, the pomegranate and the vine; today, wheat is the staff of life for us, even as it was for them. The humble onion and leek, the dill, mint and rue of our present day lives were also part of the every-day lives of the Bible people.

We can reach back to Bible days, through two thousand springtimes, when we plant a garden. From Eden to Gethsemane, the Bible is a book of gardens. It is with a garden that Genesis begins, and with a vision of trees bearing fruit that the book of Revelation ends. It was the king's pleasure to plant gardens and orchards, and build pools; the garden lavishly described in the Song of Solomon was one of oriental splendor. Besides the fruit and nut trees common in Palestine, Solomon's garden contained many flowering and aromatic shrubs, exotic spice plants from the Far East, and perhaps other foreign plants brought by the Queen of Sheba. From Persia and Egypt, Solomon is said to have borrowed floriculture; lilies and crocuses are mentioned among the flowers of his garden. It is described as a place of fountains and living waters, and when the wind blew the air was filled with spicy fragrance.

The average man could not afford such a garden, but he lived in a land where, during the rainy season, hillsides and valleys were gay with anemones, narcissi, hyacinths, morning-glories, pinks, geraniums, tulips, honeysuckles, lupines and poppies. The lilies of the field, the roses of the plains and deserts, oleanders, myrtle, laurel, useful kitchen herbs and spices, all flourished without cultivation. Yet it was part of the plan of the Promised Land that every man should have his garden spot. Even when in exile in Babylon, Jeremiah gave instructions to the children of Israel to "plant gardens, and eat the fruit of them"; and Amos promised that the people should plant gardens and eat fruit when Israel was restored.

A garden was essential to a man's life, and in death

he was often buried there. If gardens were sometimes
the scene of forbidden sacrifices, surviving from heathen
worship, they were also pleasant gathering-places for
friends, and places of rest for wayfarers. Jesus and His
disciples went into gardens often, to rest and pray. It
was in the Garden of Gethsemane that Jesus made his
great decision, and it was in the garden of Joseph of
Arimathea that the body of Jesus was laid in a sepulchre,
and where the weeping Mary mistook the risen Savior
for the gardener.

Plants play a deep and significant rôle in the Bible;
they are more than the background, more than the stage
setting of the drama that moves through the scriptural
pages. As they clothe the land of Palestine with a rich
and luxuriant verdure, they clothe the thoughts and
speech of the prophets and leaders of the land with rich
imagery and poetry. They are the symbols through
which spiritual ideas can be presented.

For us, the symbols can live again in growing green,
as we plant a Bible garden. Many of the trees and
shrubs mentioned in the Bible are excellent shade and
specimen trees for the home grounds or the church yard,
and the fruit trees of the Bible can be used effectively as
ornamental shrubs. The herbs of the Bible can be grown
in bowknot gardens, planted in flower beds, or used as
edgings and borders. Wheat, barley, and sorghum,
planted in clumps, are surprisingly decorative, as are
cucumber and watermelon vines when trained over a
trellis or a wall.

A pool, no matter how small, presents an opportunity
to include the water lilies, reeds and bulrushes of the
Scripture. In Bible times, water was the gardener's first

concern; "a river went out of Eden to water the garden" of Genesis, and pools and fountains provided water
for the great garden of Solomon. In figurative language,
a righteous man was a "well-watered garden."

Indoor gardeners will find that many of the Bible
plants make excellent house plants. Herbs can be potted
and grown on a window ledge. Myrtle will thrive as a
pot plant. The bitter orange is grown in pots or tubs
as an ornamental plant, as are also the fig, the bay tree,
and the date palm. A small olive plant, purchased from
a nursery, will grow in the living room or sun porch for
years, as will a small ebony, cinnamon or pistachio tree.
A seed from the "husks" of Scripture, known to us as
St. John's Bread, planted in a pot on the window sill,
will germinate and grow into a delightful house plant.
Dwarf pomegranates flower freely in the house, and
even apricots make successful pot and tub plants.

A bowl of blooming white narcissus—a "rose" of the
Bible—will make a charming room decoration, as will
also the lilies, the familiar poppy anemones of florists'
shops and gardens. The hyacinth and the crocus are
excellent for indoor forcing, and the star of Bethlehem
will grow and flower as readily indoors as out. Even
the giant reed and papyrus thrive as house plants.

Your Bible garden may be one of many plants, or it
may be limited to a bit of growing green in a single
flower pot but, grown as a reminder of special passages
in the Scriptures, it will create a very special atmosphere
and lead to ever fresh and inspiring discoveries in Bible
reading.

1

The Fig, the Olive and the Vine

T HE first plant mentioned by name in the Bible
is the fig, and it is followed closely by mention of the olive and vine. In the Garden of Eden,
Adam and Eve sewed fig leaves together in order
to hide their nakedness. Then, during the lifetime of
Noah, a dove plucked an olive leaf as a sign of the
retreating waters of the flood; and later, Noah became a husbandman, and planted the first vineyard.

It is significant that these three plants were mentioned
by name so early in the Bible story for, as time went on,
they became increasingly important. The fig, the olive
and vine were the principal fruits in each man's garden
and, with wheat, were the mainstay of the economic life
of the people. They were the bread of life, itself, and
seers and prophets, and later, Jesus, used them in parables and poetry.

The prophets used the fig, olive and vine—and the
wind, rain and storm that affected them—to express the
great spiritual message of their religion. They spoke of
religion, not in abstract phrases, but in terms of every-
day circumstances which people could understand. They
expressed God's goodness in terms of a fertile land
which yielded a bountiful crop. They spoke of the re-
ward of righteousness in terms of a rich harvest here on
earth. Sinfulness was punished by the blasting of the

fruits of the land. Will the fig tree languish and the vine mourn because the people have turned aside from God? When the prophet explained judgment in these terms, the average husbandman of Israel could not mistake his warning, for the fig and the vine were at the very basis of his living.

Later, Jesus used the same method of concreteness in his teaching, yet his use of nature and plant life had a profound significance far beyond that of the prophets. He chose the germinating seed, the growing fruit tree, the relationship between stem and branch to express the hidden workings of God and the Kingdom. This dynamic doctrine of growth and unfoldment was quite different from the Old Testament emphasis upon the abundance of the harvest to prove God's love of man.

In His symbols of the vine and fig tree, the mustard seed and the lilies of the field, Jesus chose words which would come down to us through the ages, alive as nature is alive, quick and powerful with the stirring of each new spring. Now as then, seeds sprout, trees give shade, vine branches depend upon the stem; and so familiar in our daily speech are the parables of nature that we do not realize, until we pursue all the plant passages of the Bible, how much our thinking depends upon these symbols.

Even better, of course, than just to read about the plants is to grow them. Gardeners speak a language of their own; and across the centuries, growers of fruits and grains and garden herbs share a common understanding of their craft. This understanding is one way— a pleasant and profitable way—to make the Bible page live for us today.

The religion of the Bible people was intimately bound up with the land to which God led them—a narrow strip of green, tree-clad country squeezed between the desert and the sea. The whole country was scarcely as large as our state of Vermont. From north to south—"from Dan to Beer-sheba," or as we would say "from Maine to Texas"—it was about one hundred and fifty miles long. From east to west, the country was sometimes less than twenty, never more than one hundred, miles wide. In the north were the Lebanon Mountains, to the east and south were deserts, and on the west was the Great Sea, now called the Mediterranean. The latitude of Palestine is that of our own South Carolina and northern Florida, and Jerusalem lies straight across the world from Jacksonville.

A mountain range extended from north to south, breaking the land into many lesser mountains, little hills and deep, still valleys. The mountain tops belonged to the Lord, and were places of security, for the Psalmist (*Ps. 125:2*) tells us: "As the mountains are round about Jerusalem, so the Lord is round about his people from henceforth even forever," and the "strength of the hills is his also" (*Ps. 95:4*). The mountains were to bring peace to the people, and the little hills, righteousness (*Ps. 72:3*). The little hills and valleys are as dear to our hearts today as they were to the people who lived among them so many years ago, for they skip and leap and rejoice on every side, and are as engaging and irresistible as a human personality.

On the west, the mountains and hills flattened out and sloped into the rich Maritime Plain, which hugged the coast of the Mediterranean. This plain produced

waving fields of wheat, but its flat surface was also the
route by which the temptations of the outside world
approached the people. Along this highway of all the
nations of the East, came camel caravans with worldly
goods from the countries beyond Palestine on their way
down to Egypt. And across this plain the horse-drawn
war chariots of the Egyptians, the Assyrians and other
conquerors were a threat to the tiny nation that lived
back in the hills.

In the east, the most famous river in the world made
a deep chasm through the mountains. The Jordan, born
of the melting snows of Lebanon, rushed down through
the tablelands, quickly cutting its way to a point below
sea level, and finally emptying into the Dead Sea, thirteen hundred feet below sea level. In this valley today
the thermometer often registers one hundred and thirty
degrees. From this low valley where tropical palm trees
flourished in days gone by, the eye can travel upward
toward the north, and see the snow-capped peak of Mt.
Hermon, nine thousand feet high. No country in the
world offers such contrast within so limited a space.

Extremes of temperature, ranging from the arctic
cold of mountain tops to the steaming heat of tropical
valleys, presented opportunity for the growth of plants
requiring all gradations of climate from cold to hot.
Palestine not only had an almost unbelievable variety
of native plants for a country of so small a size, but it
also offered growing conditions for many fruit trees and
other commercial crops that today are thought of as
plants of the temperate zone.

East and west, which furnish a contrast in the lives
of all of us, often meant the difference between life and

death in the Bible lands, depending upon the direction from which the wind blew. Winds, cool and wet with life-giving rain came from the west, blowing from the sea; winds, dry and hot with the scorching breath of sun and sand came from the east, blowing from the desert.

The difference between the rainy and dry seasons provided the most striking contrast of all. For six months the land had rain, for six months it suffered from drought. During the rainy season the whole land was green and the desert blossomed as the rose. During the rainless season the vegetation dried up and disappeared, leaving the whole land desolate and barren. One has only to refer to the word desolate in a Concordance to realize the effect of this season upon the prophets. Had it not been for the blessed dews that came to satisfy the thirst of the land and plants during the dry season, life would have been almost insupportable.

These contrasts of high and low, heat and cold, rain and drought were so marked that they have become a celebrated part of the poetry and prophecy of the Bible. It was these contrasts of nature which furnished the prophets with such eloquent imagery for the contrast of good and evil which exists in man.

In our own America we have great and violent contrasts, too, but they do not play a part in the daily life of each individual, because our country is so large. In the tiny land where the Children of Israel worked out their destiny, nature constructed her wonders on a small scale, so that her great variety became the personal experience of every inhabitant. It is as if the evergreen freshness of the Maine woods, the desert dryness of the Southwest, the turbulent landscape of the Rockies, the lofty grandeur of snow-capped Mt. Rainier and the flat grainfields of the Middle West were all combined in one small state.

In this spectacular world of nature, the Children of Israel had every opportunity to see the working of the hand of God. It was God who blessed them with an abundant crop, a fruitful season; it was God who sent the rain and dew of heaven to quench the thirst of the land; and it was God who withheld, who took away.

The fate of the people and the fate of the land are one. When the people are sinful, so is the land; it is defiled, polluted and barren. God withholds his blessings of rain and dew. Wells, pools and streams go dry in the terrible drought. Scorching east winds sweep across the land, blasting crops and withering all vegetation. Thunder crashes through the clouds, lightning strikes the trees and lights up great forest fires, mountains tremble with earthquakes—it is the God of Wrath punishing the iniquity of His children.

But when the people walk with God they are to inherit the land forever, and eat the fruit of it. When they know God in their hearts, His power will protect them, as the mountains protect Jerusalem; hills and valleys drop sweetness and overflow with fats when man recognizes the source of such blessings. Green pastures and still waters offer man a haven of bliss when he recognizes the Lord as his shepherd; springs and fountains spurt from every rock, representing the refreshing and sustaining power of the Holy Spirit. The seasons will bring food and gladness, even the desert will bloom, and the harvests lost during the years of the locusts will be restored. So all the prophets promised in terms that went straight to the heart of the husbandman. Joel (*2:21*), with good tidings, addresses the earth directly, bidding it rejoice. When righteousness prevails, Isaiah sees the land in a lilting mood; the mountains and hills break forth into singing, and all the trees of the field clap their hands (*Isa. 55:12*).

The people of the Bible not only connected their fate with that of the land, they identified themselves with the plants that grew upon it.

The favorite identification between man and plant is with the vine. Jesus said "I am the true vine," and identified himself with this plant which provided the inspiration for so many poetic passages in the Scriptures. Indeed, the whole nation of Israel was a vine, God's pleasant plant, which He declared should take root in the Promised Land and be no more plucked up. And in Psalms (*80:8-11*) we have the image of the vine taking root and filling the land:

Thou hast brought a vine out of Egypt:
Thou hast cast out the heathen, and planted it.
Thou preparedst room before it,
And didst cause it to take deep root, and it filled the land.
The hills were covered with the shadow of it,
And the boughs thereof were like the goodly cedars.
She sent out her boughs unto the sea,
And her branches unto the river.

The vine and the fig together became symbols of domestic security and happy family life, while the olive signified peace and prosperity. The Psalmist promised

"Thy wife shall be as a fruitful vine by the sides of thine house; thy children like olive plants round about thy table" (*Ps. 128:3*). In order to be happy even in captivity, the people were told to "plant gardens, and eat the fruit of them" (*Jer. 29:28*).

The phrase "under the vine and under the fig tree" came to have the significance we give to the word home; it meant, at once, shelter and happiness and love. In Solomon's day, "Judah and Israel dwelt safely, every man under his vine and under his fig tree, from Dan even to Beer-sheba" (*I Kings 4:25*). Prophesying peace, Micah says not only that men shall beat swords into plowshares, and learn no more of war, but that every man shall sit unafraid under his own vine and fig (*Micah 4:3, 4*). Here it may be worth noting that the condition of peace is security for the common man, fulfillment of his simple needs and his enjoyment of them, without fear.

Going further, to the idea of a world redeemed by a messiah, Zechariah says, "In that day, saith the Lord of hosts, shall ye call every man his neighbor under the vine and under the fig tree" (*Zech. 3:10*). Here, neighborliness or friendly relations with mankind become a further condition of peaceful enjoyment of life.

These promises of peace are full of poignant significance in an era when war has come once more to the farms and orchards of Palestine, when the blessings of peace are longed for, more strongly than ever before, by all the peoples of the earth. The ideal is timeless, and today, as we cultivate in our own garden spots the same vine and the same fig of Bible times, we hold the same hope for peace close to our hearts.

THE FIG

The fig tree plays its important rôle from Genesis to the Apocalypse. Its first mention is in Genesis (*3:7*); its last mention in Revelation (*6:13*), where the falling stars of heaven are compared to the fig tree casting its untimely fruit when shaken by a mighty wind. In between these references, the fig appears many times, and was one of the fruits brought back to Moses by the spies who had been sent to search the Promised Land.

Jesus mentioned the fig tree on more than one occasion. It was such a common and essential plant that any parable connected with it was bound to linger in the minds of the hearers. The parable of the unfruitful fig tree has an especial appeal for the man or woman who grows a Bible garden. In this parable, there is a fig tree growing in a vineyard. Each year the owner came to look at the tree, and each year it was without fruit. Finally, on the third year, he said to the vinedresser:

"Cut it down; why cumbereth it the ground?"

But the vinedresser could not bear to cut down the tree; he had tended it carefully all these years; he begged for one more year of grace; he would dig around its roots again, he would manure it well; if it refused to fruit after such care, then he would cut it down.

Jesus makes no explanation of the parable, but a favorite interpretation is that the fig tree stood for the Jewish nation. However, the promise of "one more chance" by divine mercy is universal in its appeal.

The full force of this parable strikes the gardener's heart, in particular. Every gardener has at some time lavished care on a faltering plant grown in the garden or on the window sill; how loath he is to discard such a plant as long as there is life in it! How eager he is to give it one more chance!

In Matthew (*21*) and Mark (*11*) there is another story of Jesus and a barren fig tree. The tree was in full leaf, but there were no figs upon it; Jesus condemned it and caused it to wither away. The gardener who watches his fig tree in spring, will notice that in the axil of each leaf there is a tiny, green fig, if the tree is going to bear fruit. If the tiny figs do not appear with the leaves, then the tree is going to be barren. The leaves will grow, and the tree may flourish, but it will bear no fruit. The fig tree which Jesus condemned was such a barren tree. Since it was in full leaf, it could rightly be expected to be full of fruit, however small. The fig tree of these passages, then, could very well symbolize a nation or an individual who pretended to be fruitful, but was not.

Fig trees, in a climate most favorable to their growth, produce two and three crops of figs a year; but the first-ripe figs and summer fruits are the most delicate and delicious, so that first-ripe fruits are used over and over again in the Bible as a figure of speech. Jeremiah compares the obedient and the disobedient people to baskets of figs: "One basket had very good figs, even like the figs that are first ripe: and the other basket had very naughty figs, which could not be eaten, they were so bad" (*Jer. 24:2*). And again, he says the disobedient are as "vile figs, that cannot be eaten, they are so evil" (*Jer. 29:17*).

The fig (*Ficus carica*) which was so important to the Bible people has come down the centuries, and in

America today commercial fig growing is an important industry. As a dooryard and garden plant, it is widely cultivated in the South and West, and is easily grown in the North when given winter protection. When grown far North it is safest to lift the plants, with good balls of earth on the roots, early in November, and keep them in a dry cellar over winter. In the region of Philadelphia and New York, fig trees may be bent to the ground and covered with earth or pine boughs. The fig is also grown as a tub plant, placed outside in summer and held over in a light, cool, cellar in winter, with occasional scant waterings. It will fruit freely when grown in tubs. Small plants can also be grown in a sunny window or sun porch.

Propagation is by seed, cuttings, layerings, suckers and grafting. Soil requirements are not exacting, for the fig will grow in almost any soil. It should not be over-potted or growth will be excessive. Good drainage is essential.

A very effective table decoration can be made by sowing fig seeds in a low fern dish or pan. Sow the seeds thickly, water the soil thoroughly, and then place in a semi-shady situation or at least not in full sun. Soon young plants will appear, and when about two or three inches high are very attractive. The leaves are dark green and glossy. These will not, of course, last indefinitely, but will remain attractive for several months.

OLIVE

The olive branch has become the traditional world-wide emblem of peace, for it was an olive branch that the dove brought back to Noah as evidence of the retreating flood and as a sign of God's abating wrath.

The olive tree was abundant in every part of Palestine, flourishing even in poor soils and in districts too dry for other fruit trees. It thrived in the long, rainless summers of endless sunshine, and its gray-green foliage clung to the tree in all seasons. In many places, it alone seemed to be alive and even flourishing when all other vegetation was dry and parched or had completely disappeared. So it was only natural that the Psalmist used it as a symbol of the righteous man who trusted in the everlasting mercy of God: "But I am like a green olive tree in the house of God: I trust in the mercy of God for ever and ever" (*Ps. 52:8*).

Olive trees grew on either side of the golden candlesticks in Zechariah's vision of the rebuilding of the Temple; they were symbolic of a perpetual supply of oil for the bowls upon the top of the candlesticks which held the lamps (*Zech. 4:3*). The olive trees appear again in Revelation (*11:4*) beside the two candlesticks which are standing before the God of the earth.

By following through all the references to oil and ointment in a Concordance, the significance of the olive tree in the life of the people, in the ritual of their religion and in their daily lives will be revealed. Every olive yard had its oil press, and the oil pressed from the ripe fruits played a major rôle in the life of the times; the oil represented the "fat of the land" and, in symbolism, the Holy Spirit. Its presence denoted gladness, and its absence sorrow. Oil was important as food, as medicine, as an article of the bath, as a token of respect and honor. As is usual in hot countries, oil was

used after a bath on hair and skin, and visitors were
anointed by the host as a special mark of welcome and
respect. Oil was used in illumination, and especially pure,
beaten oil was used in the lamps of the Tabernacle.

"Let him dip his foot in oil" is an expression for prosperity (*Deut. 33:24*), and the figure of speech comes
from the ancient custom of treading the olives in the
rock presses. Job, in reflecting upon the good days when
he enjoyed God's favor, and his children were yet about
him, uses the same symbol of prosperity but in different
words: "And the rock poured me out rivers of oil"
(*Job 29:6*).

The olive is a picturesque tree, with its trunk becoming gnarled in age, and its grayish green, willowlike
foliage making a pleasant shade. The blossoms, very
fragrant, are small and arranged in clusters; when the
tree is in full bloom, there is such a wealth of flowers
that the breeze, rippling through the trees, causes the
petals to fall like a shower of snowflakes. Eliphaz com-
menting on the vanities of an unwise man says that he
"shall cast off his flower as the olive" (*Job 15:33*).
When the olives were ripe and ready for harvest, the
olive gatherers climbed the trees to gather the crop;
but their instructions were to leave some of the fruits
on the topmost bough, and some on the lower and most
fruitful branches, so that there would be gleanings for
the poor.

The olive (*Olea europea*) thrives in our American
Southwest where the air is clear and dry. It needs a
deep, well drained soil, for its roots penetrate deeply.
Commercially, the olive is grown in California and in
parts of Florida, Arizona and New Mexico. It is propa-

gated by seed and cuttings, but the average gardener will want to buy a nursery plant of perhaps two or three years' growth. The trees are successfully grown in greenhouses, and the parishioner who owns a greenhouse will be able to have a growing plant available for special Bible plant displays.

Young olive plants may also be grown as house plants in pots, where they may thrive for a few years. They rest during winter. An olive branch, with a pottery dove perched upon it, makes a fitting decoration for the home or church room.

THE VINE

"I am the true vine," said Jesus, "and my Father is the husbandman. Every branch in me that beareth not fruit he taketh away: and every branch that beareth fruit, he purgeth it, that it may bring forth more fruit."

To illustrate His relationship and spiritual union with the disciples, Jesus continued: "I am the vine, ye are the branches: he that abideth in me, and I in him, the same bringeth forth much fruit: for without me ye can do nothing" (*John 15:1-8*).

These words, so simple, yet so profoundly spiritual in meaning, were spoken to the disciples; they have come down through the centuries and are perhaps the most frequently quoted words from the Bible about the vine. Jesus chose the vine, no doubt, to illustrate the idea of spiritual union, because it was one of the most important plants in the everyday life of the people. Surely no vinedresser working in the vineyards could fail to ponder these words, for he knew so well that the branches of the vine he tended and pruned would not bear fruit if severed from the stem through which they received their sustenance. And these words of Jesus have new force for us today if we think of them again in connection with the grapevines of our own gardens.

The prophets used all the circumstances surrounding the cultivation of the vine to illustrate God's care of His people. Israel, identified with the vine, was a vine which God planted or plucked up, according to whether or not it was fruitful. Familiarity with the details of planting and harvesting the vineyard makes us understand the imagery of the prophets in their warnings and promises.

Vines grew on the hillsides in fields that were carefully prepared to receive them. Terraces, to hold the soil from washing off the slopes, were built, and each vineyard was enclosed by a wall or hedge. Stones were gathered from the field and used in building the walls and terraces. Stone bases were constructed for watchtowers, and, in anticipation of the harvest, pits for the winepresses were dug.

Once the vines were planted, constant attention was necessary if the husbandman was to have a good crop. The ground must be ploughed or harrowed and kept clear of weeds. Walls and terraces must be kept in constant repair, especially during the rainy season. In spring, there must be careful pruning of dead and fruitless branches.

Slothful farmers did not give their vineyards enough attention. The careless vine-grower is described as a man "void of understanding," whose vineyard was all grown over with thorns and nettles, and whose wall was broken down (*Prov. 24:30-31*).

When the season of ripening grapes arrived, watchmen were put in towers in the fields to guard the fruit against harm; the vineyard must be protected from depredation by jackals, foxes, wild boars and other beasts of the field (*Sol. 2:15; Ps. 80:13*).

At the time of harvest, the owner and his family, or the hired vinedresser or grape gatherer and his family, moved into a summer house or booth that was erected in the field or beneath one of the towers; and soon the vineyards were ringing with the merry-hearted singing and shouting of the men and women, gathering the crop and trampling the grapes in the presses (*Isa. 16:10; Jer. 48:33*). But no righteous man forgot the poor and the stranger, the widow and the orphan in this time of happiness and thanksgiving. He remembered and obeyed the words of God that had been given long before (*Deut. 24:21*): "When thou gatherest the grapes of thy vineyard, thou shalt not glean it afterward: it shall be for the stranger, for the fatherless and for the widow."

Isaiah uses many references to vineyarding when he threatens the people with the judgment to come if they refuse to return to God. Perhaps he stood forth like a minstrel at a harvest celebration, for the first words of his fifth chapter are "Now will I sing to my well-beloved a song of my beloved touching his vineyard."

His beloved had a vineyard on a hill that had good soil and plenty of sunshine. He cleared the hillside of stones, planted the choicest vines, and then built a fence around the vineyard to protect it. He expected a rich harvest, so he built a tower where a watchman could sit while the young grapes were ripening, and a winepress where the juice could be pressed from the grapes.

And what happened? This vineyard which had every care lavished upon it yielded *wild* grapes!

What could you *do* with such a vineyard?

Surely there is no use to keep its wall in repair, or to waste time pruning its vines, or digging around their roots; rather let the briers and thorns take it, and let it dry up for want of rain!

Every man who heard the words of Isaiah must have been nodding his head in agreement. Isaiah had the crowd with him, and then he told them the true meaning of his song:

"For the vineyard of the Lord of hosts is the house of Israel, and the men of Judah his pleasant plant: and he looked for judgment, but behold oppression; for righteousness, but behold a cry" (*Isa. 5:7*).

In another mood, Isaiah repeats the words of the Lord, who cherishes His good vineyard:

"In that day sing ye unto her, a vineyard of red wine. I the Lord do keep it; I will water it every moment: lest any hurt it, I will keep it night and day . . . Israel shall blossom and bud, and fill the face of the world with fruit" (*Isa. 27:2, 3, 6*).

The worthlessness of Jerusalem, and its destruction, are explained by Ezekiel in terms of the vine which stands for it. The people were used to thinking of their nation as a vine, particularly chosen and selected by God, but Ezekiel tells them that they are wrong.

What is the vine tree more than any other tree?

How are its branches different from any wild tree of the forest?

Where is the fruit?

Its wood is useless; it is not even good enough to use as a pin upon which to hang a kitchen pot! Why, the vine tree, which was no good when it was whole, is now burned at both ends and more useless than ever!

The vine has been through one fire, but it is going through another until it is destroyed.

"And I will make the land desolate, because they have committed a trespass," saith the Lord God (*Ezek. 15:1-8*).

The prophet uses the vine again in a prophecy of destruction. This time the vine is plucked up in fury. The east wind blows upon it withering and scorching it, and then one of its branches catches on fire and the vine burns up (*Ezek. 19:10-14*).

Just as knowledge of the growth and cultivation of the vine helps us to understand the figurative passages in which the plant appears, so an acquaintance with the details of wine making helps us to understand many of the figures of speech which allude to the process.

The wine press, in which the harvested grapes were trod, consisted of two excavations, hewn out of solid rock on the hillside. If possible, one excavation was higher than the other, and the two were connected by a pipe or channel. The clusters of grapes, brought in baskets by the grape gatherers, were thrust into the upper vat where the treaders crushed the fruit, causing the juice to flow through the pipe and be caught in the basin below.

As the men trod the grapes they shouted with joy, for the vintage was the occasion of celebration and festivity. When the prophets wanted to warn the people of judgment they mentioned the day when such gladness would be taken away, when joy would leave the plentiful field; "and in the vineyards there shall be no singing, neither shall there be shouting: the treaders shall tread out no wine in their presses; I have made their vintage shouting to cease" (*Isa. 16:10*).

Also, the vintage shouting can lose its joy and be compared with the angry roar of the Lord: "The Lord shall roar from on high, and utter his voice from his holy habitation; he shall mightily roar upon his habitation; he shall give a shout" (*Jer. 25:30*). And because the treaders, while they work, splash their garments with rich, red juice, Isaiah (*63:2-6*) uses this circumstance to paint a picture of the terrible day of vengeance:

Wherefore art thou red in thine apparel,
And thy garments like him that treadeth in the winefat?

I have trodden the winepress alone;
And of the people there was none with me:
For I will tread them in mine anger,
And trample them in my fury;
And their blood shall be sprinkled upon my garments,
And I will stain all my raiment.
For the day of vengeance is in mine heart,
And the year of my redeemed is come.
And I looked, and there was none to help;
And I wondered that there was none to uphold:
Therefore mine own arm brought salvation unto me;
And my fury, it upheld me.
And I will tread down the people in mine anger,
And make them drunk in my fury,
And I will bring down their strength to the earth.

Fermentation of the juice, in the climate of Palestine, began almost immediately. The liquid became foamy, and soon the action became violent, continuing so for about a week. During this first fermentation, the juice was kept in jars and vats, and then transferred to other jars and to strong wine skins. Dregs called "lees" collected in the bottom of any container holding the new wine. Sometimes the wine was permitted to rest on the lees to gather strength and flavor, and then was carefully strained before it was drunk. Most of the wine, however, was not permitted to remain on the lees because often it not only failed to improve, but even degenerated.

The custom of transferring the wine from vessel to vessel, or of permitting it to rest upon the lees, was used, effectively, in figures of speech. "Moab hath been at ease from his youth, and he hath settled on his lees, and hath not been emptied from vessel to vessel, neither hath he gone into captivity: therefore his taste remained in him, and his scent is not changed" (*Jer. 48:11*). "I will search Jerusalem with candles, and punish the men that are settled on their lees" (*Zeph. 1:12*). "And in this mountain shall the Lord of hosts make unto all people a feast of fat things, a feast of wines on the lees, of fat things full of marrow, of wines on the lees well refined" (*Isa. 25:6*).

The vigorous action of the new wine was referred to in various ways in both the Old and New Testament. Elihu, the youngest of Job's friends, respectfully waiting for the older men to refute Job's arguments, finally reached a point where he could constrain his speech no longer. The spirit which moved him to speak was like "wine which hath no vent; it is ready to burst like new bottles" (*Job 32:19*). And Jesus said: "Neither do men put new wine into old bottles: else the bottles break, and the wine runneth out, and the bottles perish: but they put new wine into new bottles and both are preserved" (*Matt. 9:17*).

The vine and the winepress continue as symbols through all the books of the Scriptures and finally play their part in Revelation where the vintage again becomes a symbol of terror rather than joy. The angel thrusts his sickle on the earth, gathering the clusters of grapes that are fully ripe. The fruit is cast "into the great winepress of the wrath of God. And the winepress was trodden . . . and blood came out . . ." (*Rev. 14:19, 20*). In the stirring Battle Hymn of the Republic, Julia Ward Howe made poetic use of the "grapes of wrath," a phrase more recently reminiscent of John Steinbeck's famous novel, *The Grapes of Wrath*.

The vine can be used in our lives today as the visible symbol of so many different Bible passages, that surely no Bible garden will be complete without a grapevine of some kind. The grapevine of the Bible is known botanically as *Vitis vinifera* and it produces the best wine grape in the world. It was introduced into this country many years ago, and has become the basis of a successful wine industry on the Pacific Coast. This species grows easily also in Idaho, parts of Arizona and in southern Nevada and Utah; on the West coast it has run wild. It is not grown commercially in the East, but the individual gardener, by giving it special attention and winter protection, can grow the species. Today there are many varieties of *Vitis vinifera,* and they have a wide range of adaptation. Many of our native American grapes have been hybridized with *Vitis vinifera*.

Vitis vinifera is raised extensively as a hot-house grape and under glass.

A grapevine is a grapevine, however, and all look so much alike that no one but a botanist would object to a Bible garden where the biblical grapevine is represented by one of our native species.

In growing any grapevine out of doors, it is best to secure small vines of several years' growth, and train them on a trellis, over a wall or over an arbor which shelters a path or terrace. Table grapes and seedless grapes of *Vitis vinifera* are shipped to markets in the East and North, and can be used effectively in table decorations and other ways for church entertainments. Arrangements of fig and grape leaves in combination with their fruits may become the symbol of domestic peace and happiness at family and church festivities.

Sycomore-fig. Amos was a "gatherer of sycomore fruit."

2

Fruit of the Land

THE most famous fruit tree of the Bible is not mentioned where many readers expect to find it, in the book of Genesis. We think of the apple tree as the tree of knowledge because tradition has made it so, but the Eden history fails to name the fruit eaten by Eve.

Apples do appear in a number of other Old Testament books, however. In Proverbs, a word fitly spoken is compared to apples of gold. In the Song of Solomon the bride compares the bridegroom to the excellence of an apple tree. He is as an "apple tree among the trees of the wood," his shadow is a great delight, and his fruit is sweet to taste. But the Hebrew word *tappuach*, translated as apple, was used to mean *any* fruit; it could, therefore, be the fruit of an apricot or an orange tree, a citron or a quince tree, or any other fruit of the land. Most students of Bible botany agree that the apple of the Bible passages was the apricot, believed to have flourished in Palestine in those days as it does today. Some authorities hold that the golden apples were oranges, others that they were quinces, but no one argues that they were the fruit which we know as apples.

This disposes of one of the controversies which long perplexed readers who felt that they must accept or reject the Scriptures as translated. Gardeners the world over wondered how the apple trees of northern climates, out of place in Palestine, could there produce fruit tempting enough to fulfill the conditions of the text. Then came scholars to compare various translations and versions of Scripture, who found that the apple and other plant-names of the English Bible were baffling puzzles. Was the rose of Sharon a true rose, a bulbous plant, or something different from either? When Isaiah said, "The desert shall blossom as the rose," did he refer to a flower of the Rose or the Lily family? The Alexandrian translators called this particular rose a lily, the Chaldean and Arabic translators called it a narcissus. Others thought it a mallow, a crocus, an amaryllis, a tulip or an anemone.

Critical examination of the written texts was not a challenge to the truth of the Bible or a denial of its divine revelation. It was a sincere effort to correct the mistakes made by human frailty in the years when the Word of God passed through many different hands and tongues. But study of the texts was not enough to clear up confusion about the identity of the plants mentioned, since sometimes the Hebrew and Greek names had no English equivalent, or their meanings were ambiguous. It was not until botanists came along to help that the Bible scholars were able to find satisfactory answers to some of their more puzzling questions. About the middle of the eighteenth century, the great botanist, Linnaeus, suggested that the land of Palestine be studied to see which plants were growing there. He was convinced that particular plants were limited to particular parts of the world; therefore, the plants that were native to Palestine were probably not the same plants that were native to western Europe. This is such a commonplace idea to us today that it seems strange that less than two hundred years ago it had yet to be proved.

Followers of Linnaeus, embarking for Palestine to make a study of the flora, ushered in a new epoch in the study of Bible plants. Later, many botanists and botanically minded churchmen explored the area, and studied the plants of the Holy Land. Then by comparing the Bible plant-names and passages with the growing plants themselves, the etymologists and botanists were able to settle many matters of controversy that previously had seemed almost hopeless of solution.

As this acquaintance with the countryside has cleared up verbal mysteries, so the spiritual meaning of the Scriptures can be clarified by actual reference to the land and what grew upon it. Interest in growing Bible plants will, therefore, lead far beyond pleasure in the beauty of the plants themselves, and to a richer understanding of many passages of Scripture. While the fig, the olive and the vine may be mentioned more frequently by name than are the pomegranate, date-palm, sycomore-fig and other fruits of this chapter, they were all included in passages concerning the fruit of the land. All of the trees that were good for food, were blessings of God. The promise of prosperity was that the "land shall yield her increase, and the trees of the field shall yield their fruit" (*Lev. 26:4*).

Fruit trees, often referred to as "trees of the field" to distinguish them from the trees of the forest, were so greatly prized by the Hebrews that the law forbade the destruction of any fruit tree, even though it might be that of the enemy. The Mosaic law was very specific on this subject: "When thou shalt besiege a city . . .

in making war against it . . . thou shalt not destroy
the trees thereof by forcing an axe against them: for
thou mayest eat of them . . . for the tree of the field
is man's life . . . Only the trees which thou knowest
that they be not trees for meat, thou shalt destroy and
cut them down" (*Deut. 20:19-20*). And the prophets,
when predicting doom, could hardly picture a more terrible fate than that of the withering of all the "trees
of the field." Joel (*1:12*) says: "The vine is dried up,
and the fig tree languisheth; the pomegranate tree, the
palm tree also, and the apple tree, even all the trees
of the field, are withered: because joy is withered away
from the sons of men."

Any tree yielding fruit may become for us the symbol
of the godly man: "And he shall be like a tree planted by
the rivers of water, that bringeth forth his fruit in his
season; his leaf also shall not wither; and whatsoever
he doeth shall prosper" (*Ps. 1:3*).

Our own fruit trees can symbolize for us the tree of
life, which plays its part from Genesis to Revelation.
In Ezekiel the tree of life becomes the symbol for the
picture of the ideal state and the Messianic age. Ezekiel
uses again the Genesis symbol of the life-giving waters;
he describes the healing river and the trees beside it
as a convincing vision of heaven. The evergreen trees
bear nourishing fruit, and are superior to the vagaries
of weather or season, growing forever on the banks of
the life stream which flows from the sanctuary of God.
This imagery is to reappear in John's picture of the
New Jerusalem, where we have the tree of life restored
with the blessed life of Eden (*Rev. 22:1, 2, 14*).

The tree of life, as a symbol, is understood by many

Bible scholars to be the promise of immortality of the individual, rooted in earth but reaching to heaven and bearing perfect fruit there: "To him that overcometh will I give to eat of the tree of life, which is in the midst of the paradise of God" (*Rev. 2:7*).

APPLE

The golden apples of the Bible grow in our modern gardens and are known to us as apricots, quinces, oranges and citrons. These fruits were eaten by the Bible people, and the green leaves on the branches of the trees cast a pleasant shade for which the people of the Holy Land were properly grateful.

The apricot (*Prunus armeniaca*) makes a handsome ornamental tree for the home garden. It is grown commercially for its fruits on the Pacific Coast and in parts of the Rocky Mountain region, but as an ornamental its range extends all through the South and in the East as far as Massachusetts, although it is also grown commercially in New England and New York. Its range coincides with that of the peach.

Apricot flower buds open early, but if you plant your tree on a northern slope or on the north or west side of a building, or where it will be shaded by taller trees to the eastward, the buds may be retarded until too late to be nipped by frost. The early pink blossoms enhance the beauty of this tree, which is always attractive for its form and foliage.

Early fall, when the plants first become dormant, is the best time to transplant apricots, although spring planting is often preferred in the East. Budded or grafted one-year-old trees are very satisfactory for planting because they may be trained as desired. A number of varieties are available from nurserymen, so that you may choose the kind which will fit best into your garden or landscape scheme. Mulching around this tree, and all fruit trees, during summer is good practice to keep down weeds and to conserve moisture.

As a house plant, the apricot may be grown in a pot or tub, and plunged into the open ground during summer. As a house plant or outdoor plant, it likes a rather dry soil and will die if water is permitted to stand around the roots.

Single specimens of apricot trees rarely produce fruit, although they flower beautifully. Cross pollination seems to be necessary if trees are to fruit abundantly.

The quince (*Cydonia oblonga*) is widely grown in New England, in most of the Middle West and in the West. It is small, with crooked branches, and can be trained to grow either as a bush or as a small tree. It is slow growing and shallow rooted, and does best in a heavy, moist soil. One or two-year-old trees are preferred for planting in fall or spring, although it can also be propagated from hardwood cuttings and from seed. The necessary pruning consists of removing suckers and thinning the top if the branches become too crowded. The tree is handsome both during its flowering period, and during its period of fruit. The golden apples are attractive to look at. As quince jelly, they can take their place as a Bible product at a church bazaar.

The bitter orange (*Citrus aurantium*) is widely used in this country as a propagating stock, but seldom planted for its fruit by commercial fruit growers. As an ornamental tree, it takes readily to life in pots or tubs, and may be started from seed. Its fruit is preferred to that of the sweet orange in making marmalade. The petals yield a valuable perfume, and the peel is often candied. This "sour orange" is naturalized in Florida, where it was brought in the early days by the Spaniards.

The citron (*Citrus medica*) is a small tree with long, irregular branches and short, stiff thorns. In this country it is raised principally as a greenhouse plant. The peel of its large, lemonlike fruit is candied and widely used in confectionery and cakes.

The soil for both orange and citron should be of moderately heavy loam, with a liberal addition of decayed manure and sufficient sand to make the soil porous. When potting, ram the soil firmly. The potted or tubbed plants should be placed in full sun, out of doors, during the summer.

Husks

In the famous story of the Prodigal Son, told in the fifteenth chapter of Luke, there was a father who had two sons. The younger asked for his inheritance, which he received and soon spent in riotous living. When he had no money or food left, he hired himself out as a keeper of swine. And because he had no bread, he longed to eat the husks which were fed to the swine.

The husks were the beans of the carob tree, a lovely evergreen which reaches a height of thirty feet. It has glistening leaves, small yellow flowers, and thick, flattened pods from six to ten inches long and an inch wide. These pods are in the form of a curved sickle, and the pealike seeds are embedded in a pleasantly flavored, mucilaginous, saccharine pulp used today, as in Bible times, for feeding swine and cattle. The sweet pulp is ground up with the pods and used for making candies. The dried pods are sold in street markets in Northern cities where they are called St. John's Bread. This name has been given the pods because they were once thought to have been pods of the locust tree, the locusts eaten by John the Baptist in the wilderness. However, many Bible authorities believe that these locusts were insects of that name—looked upon favorably as food in the East.

The carob tree (*Ceratonia siliqua*) is now widely distributed in warm countries. It was first introduced into America on a large scale in the 1850's. About eight thousand plants grown from seed in Washington were distributed during the spring of 1860 in the Southern States. Their range of climate is about the same as that of the orange. The carob grows easily in the mild climates of the Gulf States, especially in the coastal regions of Texas, the southern parts of New Mexico and Arizona, and most of California. If given protection in winter for several years, the range of the tree can be considerably extended.

It is grown from seed and cuttings, but is difficult to transplant and will not live unless moved with a ball of earth around the roots. The plants are often started in pots, then lifted out and set in the locations where the trees are to grow. The carob is a very slow grower and can be encouraged to live in a pot for quite a while, and so for the first several years of its life it makes an engaging house plant. The seeds are usually slow to germinate. A convenient way to start a carob plant is to place a seed in the soil of a pot already containing a plant whose life will be shorter than that of the carob. In this way the seed—and later the seedling—receives water and care during the time when it might otherwise be neglected if started in a pot all its own.

Nuts

Almonds, walnuts and pistachios are the "nuts" of the Bible, although the almond is the only one mentioned by name. Almonds and pistachio nuts were among the presents taken to Egypt by the sons of Jacob, when they went to buy "corn." The walnut tree is supposed to have grown in the garden of Solomon: "I went down into the garden of nuts to see the fruits of the valley" (*Sol. 6:11*). Nuts were important as food and oil during Bible times, as they are today.

The Hebrew word " shâked" is translated "almond," and means, literally, "to watch for." The Hebrews watched for the beautiful pink or white almond flowers as a sign of the awakening of spring. Because of its early flowering habit, a branch of an almond tree became a symbol of the early fulfillment of a promise. A conversation between the Lord and Jeremiah (*1:11, 12*) illustrates this symbolism.

"Jeremiah, what seest thou?" the Lord asked.

"I see a rod of an almond tree," Jeremiah replied.

"Thou hast well seen: for I will hasten my word to perform it," said the Lord. In the original Hebrew, there is a play upon words linking almond to the ever-wakeful, ever-watchful quality of God. The Moffatt translation of the Bible gives "almond" in this passage

as "wake-tree." The quality of wakefulness is an attri-
bute of God clearly expressed in Psalms (*121:4*) : "He
that keepeth Israel shall neither slumber nor sleep."

The almond is of such ancient cultivation that its
native land is uncertain, but it is thought to be native
to western India and Persia and to have spread west-
ward in very early times so that it was common in
Palestine during the days of Jacob. The "hazel boughs"
which are mentioned in the King James version in the
story of Jacob and the ring-streaked cattle (*Gen.
30:37*) are believed today to be the boughs of an
almond tree; and many other translations of the Bible
give almond, instead of hazel. Almonds are mentioned
by name when Jacob tells his sons to take gifts with
them to Egypt: "And carry down the man a present, a
little balm, and a little honey, spices and myrrh, nuts,
and almonds" (*Gen. 43:11*).

Later, when the descendants of Jacob moved to
Egypt, it is possible that they carried the almond tree
with them. At any rate, it must have become common in
Egypt during those times, because, when the Israelites
escaped to the wilderness, there is evidence that they
were thoroughly familiar with the tree. The almond
does not grow in the desert, so that when the Israelites
adopted its flowers and fruits as models for ornament-
ing the bowls of the golden lampstands (*Ex. 25:33-
36*), it must have been from memory of the tree which
they had known in Egypt.

It was in the wilderness, too, that the rod of Aaron
burst into bud and blossom and yielded almonds (*Numb.
17:8*). This was a sign from God which struck awe into
the hearts of the people and encouraged them to accept

The olive tree, symbol of the fat of the land and the light of the Temple, thrives in the American Southwest.

Spiritual symbols can live
again in growing green...

This fig tree ripens its fruit
in an 8 inch pot.

the leadership of Moses, and Aaron and his family. Here, again, the almond rod is used in connection with the fulfillment of God's word.

The almond (*Prunus communis* or *Amygdalus communis*) is a peachlike tree with gray bark which grows to a height ranging from ten to twenty-five feet. It blooms very early in this country even as it did in Palestine, so that its buds are liable to be nipped by frost, thus lessening the tree's suitability for commercial growing in the East. In California and in the states of the Southwest, it is grown commercially for its nuts.

Its large flowers, sometimes pink and sometimes white, make it desirable in the home garden, and it is hardy all the way east and north to Pennsylvania and Long Island. There are dwarf and weeping forms which are merely varieties of the original Bible species, although these horticultural varieties have, no doubt, been produced since Biblical times.

You may start your tree from seed, or from one-year-old nursery stock, in a light, well drained loam. If you wish to have a crop of nuts, purchase grafted or budded stock. Plant the tree in fall or spring, according to the severity of climate. This tree makes a strong and rapid root growth and is more tolerant of drought than any other of our leading deciduous fruit trees. This tree, like the apricot, must stand in well drained soil; it will not live if water stands on its roots.

The pistachio nuts, mentioned with almonds in the verse above, were from the tree *Pistacia vera*. It grew in many localities in Palestine and thrives today in the United States through the Middle West, the South, and in California. It is a dry climate tree, hardier than the fig and olive. In planting this tree in the garden or in a pot, it is best to secure nursery stock. If you wish to start a plant from seed, however, soak it first in lye water and then rub with burlap or other rough material to remove the pulp.

Pistachio nuts are a valuable article of commerce and, even where the tree is not available, the nuts may be used to represent the tree in a Bible plant display.

The walnut tree that grew in the garden of Solomon, and in other localities of Palestine, was the Persian walnut. As the Persian walnut, it was introduced into England about three hundred and fifty years ago. When it traveled later to this country, it became the English walnut. But whether you know it as the Persian or the English walnut, it is still the species of the Bible land, *Juglans regia.* It produces a fine shade, and is hardy as far North as Philadelphia. It is widely grown in the East from Pennsylvania to Georgia, and is well-known in the West. It grows best in moderately moist, rich soil and prefers well drained hillsides. English walnuts are always available in the market, and the nuts could be used in a church exhibit of Bible plants if the trees themselves are not available to lend their branches.

PALM

Palm trees were associated with rejoicing. On the first day of the Feast of the Tabernacles, the Hebrews were commanded to take branches of palms and other trees and rejoice. "And ye shall take you on the first day the boughs of goodly trees, branches of palm trees, and the boughs of thick trees, and willows of the brook; and ye shall rejoice before the Lord your God seven days" (*Lev. 23:40*).

The date-palm grew in Egypt, where it was the largest native tree in the land, because no forest or timber trees were native in rainless Egypt. The palm also grew in the desert oases, and in the hot valleys of Palestine near springs or rivers. In the desert, the palm trees in the distance heralded the presence of water to the wanderer; the glimpse of palm trees was a welcome sight after a day's hot journey across the "howling wilderness" and a cause for great rejoicing. When the Children of Israel came to the oasis of Elim, they had been wandering in the wilderness for three days without water. The discovery of this oasis was so important that the actual number of its wells and palm trees was recorded in Exodus (*15:27*). No wonder they called the oasis Elim or Sacred Trees.

The stems and leaves of palm trees were used as designs for architectural decorations in Solomon's Temple, and on the walls of the house were carved figures of cherubim and palm trees (*I Kings 6:29*).

The large leaves were used in ancient times, and are used today, to cover the roofs and sides of houses. Mats, baskets, and even dishes are made of them. The fruit, borne in immense drooping clusters among the leaves, is still the chief article of food for innumerable tribes of Arabia and Africa.

To the Children of Israel and to most of us moderns, the phrase, "branches of palm trees," seems perfectly correct. But the botanists point out that, although the leaves themselves are branchlike, the palm, botanically speaking, does not have branches; the leaves are attached directly to the main stem.

The date-palm (*Phoenix dactylifera*) is grown commercially for its fruit in Texas, Arizona and California, and in irrigated sections of the hot and arid Southwestern states. It is planted for ornament and shade in gardens and parks. This plant, common in many gardens, is often the product of seeds taken from commercial dates bought in a store.

Outdoors, palms should be planted in a somewhat protected position and sheltered from too intense sun, as well as from cold winds. Although palms are usually thought of in connection with sandy places, they need plenty of water, especially in the dry season. In the deserts of their native land, they may grow where there is no apparent sign of water, but their presence denotes water at the roots.

Over most of the country, palms are best known as tub or house plants, and they are unequaled for resistance to neglect. They require relatively little sun and grow surprisingly well in hot, dry rooms. They should not be subjected to sudden, cold drafts from an open window or door; this causes the leaves to turn brown and eventually to drop. They should be watered thoroughly whenever necessary, but sparingly during the winter months. To keep the leaves free from dust and soot, sponge them frequently with clear water.

In summer, tub-palms should be moved to shady and sheltered positions out of doors. The large tubs can be hidden by lower growing plants, or plunged halfway into the ground. The chief danger is from sun and wind, and a sheltered position on the north side of a building, or under the shade of trees, is the best spot for the palm's summer vacation.

The date-palm should be potted in spring in a soil consisting of about three parts loam, one part decayed cow manure, and some sand.

As a novelty, plant date seeds from a commercial package of dates in an indoor window box. They sometimes do not germinate for several months. The young plants are interesting to watch, but are of no use as ornamentation.

POMEGRANATE

Pomegranates were very important in the life of the ancients, not only as food but as a motif in artistic design. They were prized for their juice which was made into a spiced wine, and they were among the fruits mentioned by the Israelites in the desert when they were complaining to Moses about the good things they had left behind in Egypt. When the spies entered the Promised Land, they came back with tales of its fruitfulness, and pomegranates were among the fruits mentioned.

Many of the references, however, are to the use of the form of the fruit in ornamentation. As a decorative motif, it was to the Hebrews what the lotus bud was to the Egyptians. It was a favorite design in embroidery, and the skirts of Aaron's priestly robes were embroidered with pomegranates of blue, purple, and scarlet twined linen. In between each pomegranate flower hung a bell, a shape which came from the flower (*Ex. 39:24-26*). And the brass ornamentation on the Temple was of pomegranate design (*II Kings 25:17*), and a

hundred pomegranates hung from each of the chains
that were put on the heads of the pillars (*II Chron.
3:16*). The chains were probably wreaths of chain work
that were carved on the capitals. In II Chronicles
(*4:13*), the description is of "four hundred pomegranates on the two wreaths; two rows of pomegranates on
each wreath, to cover the two pommels of the chapiters
which were upon the pillars." Although no mention is
made of it in the Bible, the crownlike calyx of the
pomegranate is believed to have been the inspiration
for the crown worn by kings. The pomegranate was an
emblem of fertility, because of the many seeds borne
within the fruit, and it was regarded as a sacred plant
by the heathen. Many commentators are of the opinion
that the idolatrous temple called the house of Rimmon,
in Assyria, was devoted to the worship of the pomegranate. Rimmon is the Hebrew word which has been
translated pomegranate, and this word appears in the
names of various places. A locality having Rimmon in
its name would mean something like "Pomegranate-
ville" to us.

The handsome red, yellow, or white, bell-shaped blossoms must have been highly prized in the Hebrew's
garden of fruit trees. The fruit, about the size of an
apple, has a hard rind which is red or yellowish when
ripe.

The pomegranate (*Punica granatum*) is hardy as far
north as Washington and Baltimore. A popular hedge
plant in the South, it is a successful pot and tub-plant
in the North. Its natural growth is bushy, but it can be
trimmed into a small tree, from fifteen to twenty feet
tall. The leaves are glossy green with red veins, and the

branches are slender, twiggy and sometimes thorny. The orange-red flowers have crumpled petals and numerous stamens. The fruit ripens in September.

Plants are propagated by seed, by hardwood cuttings planted in open ground during February, and by softwood cuttings planted during the summer. When seeds are sown, the seedlings, like those of many other plants, do not reproduce the variety from which they come. About the only successful method of obtaining the same variety is by cuttings which are made in February or March while the plants are at rest. They root about as readily as the willow.

The pomegranate can be grown from seeds or cuttings as a house plant, but a dwarf variety has been especially developed for the indoor garden. These can be grown from seed, and will furnish a few flowers the first year, and a plant two or more years old will bloom abundantly.

In this country, pomegranates are grown mostly as ornamental plants; some varieties are grown for flowers only, and are non-fruiting. In Florida, Georgia, Louisiana and other Southern States, the pomegranate is often grown commercially for its fruit, which is shipped to Northern markets.

SYCAMINE

Jesus said that if a man had faith, even as little as a grain of mustard seed, he could say to the sycamine tree, "Be thou plucked up by the root, and be thou planted in the sea," and it should obey. This sycamine, (*Luke 17:6*), is believed by most authorities to refer to the mulberry tree—to the black mulberry (*Morus nigra*) which is very common in Palestine.

In the United States the black mulberry grows in the South and on the Pacific Coast, and has even run wild along roadsides. In New England and New York, it is not hardy except in protected places. It will thrive in any well drained soil where the winters are not too cold, and is a picturesque tree with large luxuriant dark, dull-green leaves. It is easily increased by cuttings; few fruits can be expected, however, before the mulberry is fifteen years old. It is not especially ornamental grown in a pot, but could be included in a collection of Bible plants.

SYCOMORE

The sycomore of the Bible is not the tree which we call sycamore in America, but a fig tree, sometimes called "Pharoah's fig."

The sycomore-fig (*Ficus Sycomorus*) grew in Palestine and Egypt. It produces figs on all parts of the tree; they are borne on the trunk and on old limbs as well as upon new branches. The fruit is smaller than that of the ordinary fig (*Ficus carica*) and is inferior in quality, although it was commonly used as food in Bible days. It was one of the largest and most common trees in Egypt, and many of the mummy coffins which have been discovered are made of its wood.

The tree is strong and sturdy and grows to a height of from thirty to forty feet. It has a short main trunk that divides into many branches near the ground, and so is easily climbed. It is the tree which Zacchaeus, the publican, climbed so that he could see Jesus as he passed through Jericho (*Luke 19:1-7*).

Before he began to preach, the prophet Amos was a "herdman and a gatherer of sycomore fruit" (*Amos 7:14*). Most commentators interpret this phrase to mean that Amos was employed in making incisions in the sycomore fruit so that the fruit would mature. An interesting Bible study lesson can be built around this tree, particularly in connection with Amos. His occupation as a herdsman and tender of sycomore figs indicates his simple life. His work was that of a poor man and so he knew what the poor of his time were suffering in the reign of Jeroboam II, who had brought wealth and power to Israel, luxury and intemperance to the rich. To Amos it was clear that drought, locusts, famine and pestilence were sent by God to warn the people to change their ways.

Amos, the simple country man who had tended the sycomores which were the food of the poor people, used the imagery of farm life when he spoke. He reminded the people that God had withheld the rain, that the crops had been smitten with blasting and mildew; and "when your gardens and your vineyards and your fig trees and your olive trees increased, the palmerworm devoured them: yet have ye not returned unto me, saith the Lord." In his last words, when the restoration is promised, he speaks the words of the Lord, promising that the "mountains shall drop sweet wine," and the children of Israel shall "also make gardens, and eat the fruit of them."

The sycomore-fig grows in southern Florida. It is too

tender for the ordinary garden, but because of its importance to the people of Bible times, it should be grown in a Bible-plant collection. The plant should be kept in a comparatively small pot, in a soil consisting of sandy loam and leafmold.

3

Trees of the Lord

WHEN the Children of Israel entered the Promised Land, it was already a land of wide cultivation, of "wheat and barley, of figs and vines, and pomegranates." But native trees remained; there were groves of oaks and terebinth on hillsides and mountain tops, woodlands of poplars and plane trees, forests of cedar and pine in the Lebanon mountains and on the tablelands east of Jordan. Thickets of myrtle and bay trees grew on slopes and along watercourses; masses of oleanders bloomed in the hot valleys along the edges of streams. In rocky, barren places where there was too little soil or water to support a tree, the bushy desert retam or broom softened the landscape.

Since trees must have water, their presence indicated that the rain, dew or snows of heaven provided them with the living waters which they needed to keep alive. The woodlands presented a picture of year-round prosperity in contrast to the appearance of other uncultivated land which was green only during the rainy season. If, in our own country, we could walk out of the desert of the Southwest into the evergreen woods of Maine, we could experience the full force of the contrast which took place in the Hebrew's life.

Forest trees were truly the trees of the Lord (*Ps. 104:16*). Fruit trees flourished in the gardens of men

43

and with the help of men; but the woodlands of oak and cedar were nourished only by God. Thus the planting of trees in the wilderness became a symbol of God's marvelous power on earth. Isaiah used the idea of planting trees in the desert as an everlasting sign of His glory: "And I will plant in the wilderness the cedar, the shittah tree, and the myrtle, and the oil tree; I will set in the desert the fir tree, and the pine, and the box tree together: that they may see, and know, and consider, and understand together, that the hand of the Lord hath done this" (*Isa. 41:19, 20*).

What symbol of the Lord's ability to bless the land of his people with abundance could have been more effective? To clothe the desert with glorious vegetation, to transform the dry places into woods of fragrant evergreen, was a vision of heaven on earth. Any man finding a welcome shelter from the heat in the cool depths of a grove, breathing the aromatic air of the pine hills or the scent of cedar in the sun, could understand the prophet's promise of a better world.

Trees not only represented the power of God on earth, they also were used to express the idea of man's immortality, and stood as the symbol of the righteous man. Jeremiah (*17:6-8*) compared the righteous man, who drew his strength from God, to a "tree planted by the waters"—a tree which "shall not see when heat cometh, but her leaf shall be green; and shall not be careful in the year of drought, neither shall cease from yielding fruit." This dependence of trees upon water is the parallel of man's dependence upon God.

The simile of tree and water, or tree and river, is used in Psalms (*1:3*) as well as in the book of Jere-

miah, and was developed further in the prophecy of
Ezekiel. The forty-seventh chapter of Ezekiel is an
interesting study in the symbolism of water and all life
on land, because trees, men and animals are shown to be
dependent upon the life-giving waters, or Holy Spirit.
In our lives today, this symbolism is as impressive as in
Bible days; for now every school child recognizes the
essential relationship between land and water. Here
science and religion, with poetry, meet on common
ground.

In the service of God and man, the trees of the
Promised Land had valuable uses. The shittah or acacia
trees of the desert were used in building the Tabernacle, as was the Ark of the Covenant which the wan-
derers carried with them into the Land of Promise. The
cedar, pine and box were used in building the famous
Temple of Solomon: the "glory of Lebanon shall . . .
beautify the place of my sanctuary" (*Isa. 60:13*).

Cypress, cedar, oak and other woods were felled for
ships' timber and masts; the Israelites themselves were
not a seafaring people, but there are various references
to the use of trees in ship building. Ezekiel (*27:5,6*)
speaks of the port of Tyre and its merchant shipping,
with masts made from the cedars of Lebanon and oars
cut from the oaks of Bashan.

The resins, oils, fragrant leaves and flowers were
used in making the spicery and perfumery of the times.

There was also a dark and shameful side to man's
attitude toward trees in the ancient days of Bible nar-
rative. When the Children of Israel came into the Promised Land, it was occupied by heathen who worshiped
trees; but this heathen worship of the groves carried

with it a sense of primitive fear, of magic and mystery, and perhaps furnished cover for evil practices. The heathen folk also made idols of wood, setting their altars to these false gods on every high hill, and worshiping a different idol "under every green tree."

Hebrew prophets, blasting idol worship in utter scorn, pointed out that idols cannot be sacred because they are the work of men's hands. Isaiah, in his forty-fourth chapter, ridicules the man who goes into the forest and selects a good cedar, or a cypress or an oak—a tree which God has planted, or the rain of heaven nourished. Then he hews it down, burns part to warm himself and to bake bread, and makes a graven image of what is left; he falls down and worships the stump. What an absurd man to deceive himself in this way! In his folly, the idolater has forgotten that the tree and the ashes and the food all came from the one and only God.

The gods of the groves were diverse powers to be appealed to or appeased, but the Hebrews, wandering in the barren desert, had learned over and over again that God was one, the ruler of all nature; from him came the trees, the water, the clouds, the quail, the manna; every part of nature with which they had experience was subject to the one God. They saw that a power far above the tallest of the trees timed the seasons, the rainfall, the winds, and the weather upon which the scheme of vegetable life depended. In time, their prophets declared that this divine power was superior also to the elements, controlled the lightning and held "the wind in his fists" (*Prov. 30:4*). This was the great concept of the Hebrew religion, its difference from the worship of Baal and the older gods of tribal worship. The Children of Israel were the first to see all of nature as a part of and subject to God; they were the first to explain the whole universe as an expression of the one God.

True, the Children of Israel were only human and sometimes very foolish. They were constantly falling in with heathen ways, enflaming themselves with idols under every green tree (*Isa. 57:5*). They forgot the unseen power which was able to consume the wood of Baal's sacrifice (*I Kings 18:38*). They could be caught burning incense to heathen gods, on altars hidden in their own gardens which God had given them (*Isa. 65:3*). But again and again they were called back to the true worship by the reminder that gardens and trees were the gifts of God, subject, like man, to one universal law.

The spiritual meaning of the passages where trees are mentioned is clear, but the identity of the specific trees of the Bible has aroused great controversy. The Hebrew words for various kinds of trees are not directly translatable into such English names as oak or pine. In Hebrew text, trees were spoken of as thick trees, strong trees, mighty trees, groves of trees. Cypress comes from a word whose root means to be hard. Pine comes from a word which has a root signifying to revolve. It is only natural then that the translators have interpreted these words in different ways. The word translated as heath in the King James version has been translated in other versions not only as a plant, but sometimes as guinea hens and goats.

Box

The box tree is a hardy evergreen with a stem six or eight inches in diameter, about twenty feet in height. It grows with other evergreens in the northern part of Palestine and in the Lebanon range. These tree-clad mountains, rich-green all year round, did not show signs of the dry season as did other sections of Palestine. The rains and snows were caught and held by the roots of trees, so that the water was relinquished slowly and fed to streams, and to springs and fountains that gushed forth from the foot of the mountains. The Bible has many references to the value of Lebanon and its melting snows, and the mountains with their trees became a symbol of the greatness and beauty of life, of the grandeur of God's handiwork. Isaiah, in speaking of rebuilding the Temple in the days of the restoration, said that God's dwelling place should have in it the most precious of woods: "The glory of Lebanon shall come unto thee, the fir tree, the pine tree, and the box together, to beautify the place of my sanctuary" (*Isa. 60:13*).

But when we ask which botanical species were the trees of Isaiah's verse, the answers are many and varied. Some authorities believe that the box tree mentioned is *Buxus longifolia;* others that it is *B. sempervirens.*

The box of our gardens is of the species *B. sempervirens;* it is so similar to *B. longifolia* that it is well able to represent the tree of Isaiah's verse. The hard, close-grained wood of box is used in wood engraving and for finer wood work.

Many varieties of box are available for garden use

The rocky barren hillsides of modern Palestine were once protected against erosion by the "trees of the Lord" and a remarkable terrace system.

W. C. *Lowdermilk*

Cedar of Lebanon, masterpiece of God. This cedar thrives in the United States and is hardy as far north as Boston.

in this country. They stand pruning well and are used widely for low hedges, edgings or borders for flower beds or walks. Box is slow growing, has small, leathery leaves, inconspicuous flowers and is a real old-time, garden plant often seen in Southern, colonial gardens. It grows in any well drained soil and seems to prefer partial shade.

CEDAR OF LEBANON

Among the forest trees of the Bible, the cedar of Lebanon was king. With the lion among beasts, and the eagle among birds of the air, it took its place as a symbol of power and strength. Its stately grandeur was part of the glory of Lebanon and of all Israel, just as our giant Sequoias represent the grandest of all the trees of our continent. Although it does not attain the height of our Big Trees, the cedar of Lebanon belongs to the same family, and also attains a tremendous age. It seldom exceeds one hundred and twenty feet in height, but its wide-spreading, horizontal branches and thick trunk, sometimes eighteen feet in diameter, give it the quality of permanence and strength which made it an object of awe and reverence.

The cedars are very aromatic and the "smell of Lebanon" is one of the vivid sense impressions brought down to us in the Bible. Dramatic atmosphere is furnished when the smoke of forest fires fills the air, earthquakes make the mountains tremble, and thunder—"the God of glory thundering"—shakes the wilderness, breaking its cedars (*Ps. 29:1-11*).

The Hebrews were poets who seized upon the beauty

and magnificence of these trees to help them explain their ideas. The cedar was a powerful subject of imagery in the hands of Ezekiel, who used its greatness to rebuke the worldly of a self-confidence which relied upon man instead of God. The presumptuous man became a tall tree, lopped off in towering pride. Ezekiel, in his eloquent thirty-first chapter, warns Pharaoh of his fate in terms of a fallen cedar. Of a fair height, with spreading branches, this tree was more beautiful than any other in the garden of God; but it fell when the topmost branches soared too high above the great waters at its roots.

Although there are few groves of these cedars left today, at one time great forests of cedars covered the mountains and were used for purposes of peace and war. The most spectacular plunder of the Lebanon forests was for the building of Solomon's Temple, which was to be "exceedingly magnificent, of fame and glory throughout all countries." We are told the story of this amazing enterprise in chapters five, six and seven of the first book of Kings; in chapters twenty-eight and twenty-nine in the first book of Chronicles; in chapters one, two, three and four of the second book of Chronicles. It required seven years of back-breaking toil to complete the Temple and thirteen years more to build Solomon's private house, the house of the Forest of Lebanon, the great Porch of Judgment, and the house of Pharaoh's daughter, Solomon's favorite wife. For this work he conscripted 30,000 Israelites who were sent to Lebanon in shifts, one hundred fifty thousand laborers who were captive slaves from past wars, and three thousand three hundred officers over all.

The cedar of Lebanon (*Cedrus libani* or *C. libanotica*) has been grown in this country for many years in arboretums and botanical gardens, in parks and by many private individuals. It is an attractive shade tree to plant in the church ground or on the home property. It prefers well drained, loamy soil, and will grow in sandy clay if there is no stagnant moisture.

Small plants can be obtained from nurseries and a small plant will make a good showing in a Bible garden. It will take a number of years for it to reach shade-tree size, but if planted near shorter-lived trees in its youth, it will make a nice shrub until it grows large enough to overtop the other trees. This cedar used to be considered tender north of Washington, D. C., but many years ago the Arnold Arboretum in Boston introduced specimens from very high elevations which have successfully withstood the northern winters with no protection. Seeds of the trees have been distributed among nurserymen, and stock is now available for the public.

CEDAR WOOD

In the wilderness, the Children of Israel were given instructions to use "cedar wood" in purification ceremonies (*Lev. 14:4-6* and *Numb. 19:6*). As Bible commentators point out, the cedar wood used in the desert could not possibly have been the cedar wood of Lebanon, which was growing on mountains many miles away and unknown to the Israelites at the time. The cedar wood of these early references must have been the wood of a tree or shrub abundant in the desert, perhaps the juniper (*Juniperus Oxycedrus* or *J. phoenicia*) known to us as prickly juniper and Phoenician juniper.

These junipers are bushes, or small trees, common in dry regions in western Asia. The wood has a strong odor, and when burned with the bodies of birds, or heifers, used in the religious ceremony, the juniper fumes made the odor of burning flesh less noticeable.

These two shrubs can be grown out of doors far south in the United States. The prickly juniper is a shrub which grows to thirty feet, with linear, spreading, spiny-pointed leaves. The Phoenician juniper grows to twenty feet, with scalelike, dark bluish green leaves.

CHESTNUT

The Hebrew word armôn means naked, and although the King James version interprets this word as chestnut, other translations call this naked tree a plane tree. The outer bark of the plane tree falls off in large strips or sections giving the trunk a white and naked appearance. The plane tree (*Platanus orientalis*) flourishes in the mountains of Lebanon, and in plains and valleys along banks of streams. True chestnuts do not grow in Palestine, although one species is native in the Caucasus region of western Asia.

The word chestnut was used in the story of Jacob and the ring-streaked cattle (*Gen. 30:37*) and in Ezekiel's poem of the downfall of the mighty cedar (*Ez. 31:8*), but most authorities are agreed that the words plane tree instead of chestnut should appear in these passages. A number of translators believe that the ash tree of Isaiah (*44:14*) was a plane tree, since the ash does not grow in Palestine. Both the fir and pine of other Isaiah passages are sometimes translated plane tree. This tree was highly valued by the heathen of those days who planted groves around their dwellings, since no other tree afforded so fine a shade.

The Oriental plane tree is greatly valued by all city dwellers because it flourishes in smoke-filled, grimy cities where no other tree will live. Its habit of shedding bark enables it to peel off the soot-clogged outer skin and so to continue to breathe and flourish. This is equally true of our native plane tree (*Platanus occidentalis*), but our native species is more susceptible to disease than is *Platanus orientalis*. A hybrid (*Platanus acerifolia*), a cross between the Oriental and native plane, is widely used as a street tree in this country. The native plane would ably carry out the spirit of the Bible planting, since there is little difference in the appearance of the trees. The plane tree is often called sycamore in this country; but it should not be confused with the sycamore of the Bible, which, as we have already seen, refers to the sycamore-fig.

Plane trees can be planted near the home or in the church grounds when very young, or when full-grown, which is naturally an expensive operation. The Oriental plane grows to a height of eight feet; the hybrid plane to one hundred feet, and the native sycamore to one hundred and seventy feet.

CYPRESS

The cypress is a large, tall-growing evergreen tree which grows with the cedar and oak on Mt. Lebanon.

Although mentioned in a number of different verses in the Bible, the translators have never been able to agree about the passages in which the cypress rightfully belongs. They do agree that the cypress (*Cupressus sempervirens*) is one of the trees of the Bible, and that it sometimes may have been called box, pine, cedar or oak. Practically everyone agrees that it was the gopher wood used by Noah in building the ark (*Gen. 6:14*). Cypress wood is very hard and durable and was used by the Phoenicians and Greeks in shipbuilding, and by the ancient heathen for making idols.

This species (*C. sempervirens*), called Italian cypress, is commonly cultivated in our country in the South and West. Hardy from North Carolina to Arkansas and southward, it does best in deep, well drained, sandy loam soils, in partly shaded positions and sheltered against dry winds. The foliage is dark green, and in one variety, the form resembles the Lombardy poplar. It is propagated by seeds sown in the spring and increased also by cuttings from mature wood, taken in the fall, inserted in a sandy soil and kept in a cold frame or greenhouse during winter. Best results would come, of course, from buying nursery stock.

ELM

Elm appears but once in the King James version: "They sacrifice . . . under oaks and poplars and elms," (*Hos. 4:13*). A few commentators defend the elm (*Ulmus campestris*) as the tree of the Hosea verse; and as the tree, called teil, in the verse of Isaiah 6:13. But the great majority of students favor the terebinth (*Pis-*

tacia terebinthus) as the tree meant for elm and for teil.

The terebinth introduced by the Department of Agriculture many years ago has become established in the Southwest. It will grow in well drained situations in any climate in which the olive will grow, although it is hardier than the olive. It is a large deciduous tree, resembling an oak, particularly when leafless. The pinnately compound leaves are similar to those of an ash, but are smaller and reddish green in color. Every part of the tree contains a fragrant, resinous juice. In Palestine, it is common in rocky places and on hillsides, generally growing as a solitary tree, seldom in thickets or forests. It is a tree of large size and great longevity, so that during ancient times, it received the same veneration as did oaks and cedars. The terebinth is also called the turpentine tree, because its stem and branches yield the so-called Ohio turpentine of commerce. It is native to Gilead, and no doubt its resin formed part of the spicery which the Ishmaelites carried into Egypt from Gilead.

Many of the oak tree references in the Bible come from Hebrew words which a number of scholars believe should have been translated as terebinth. The Valley of Elah, in which David slew Goliath, is translated by many authorities as the Valley of the Terebinth, because of the numbers of terebinths that grew there.

FIR

The fir tree of the Scriptures may be a pine, cypress, juniper, or even a true fir, although most authorities seem to regard it as a pine or cypress.

The only true fir of the Lebanon region is the species *Abies cilicica;* it grows on the higher parts of Lebanon and in the mountains northward, attaining a height of from thirty to seventy-five feet. This fir is cultivated in the United States and is hardy and desirable in the Northern States. It needs a well drained soil and is most beautiful in cultivation under fifty years of age; when young it forms a dense pyramid of gray-green foliage which is extremely ornamental. It is propagated by seeds which should be planted in carefully prepared seed beds, and covered with soil to a depth equal to the thickness of the seed. Young plants appear in a few weeks and need the protection of brush screens.

The green fir tree of Hosea (*14:8*) is believed to be the stone pine (*Pinus pinea*) because it produces edible nuts. In this verse, an evergreen tree that refreshes by its shadow and sustains by its fruit becomes a symbol of God.

GREEN BAY TREE

The sweet bay, or laurel, grew in thickets and woods from the coast to the middle mountain zone in Palestine, looking prosperous in all seasons because its leathery, aromatic leaves retained their evergreen freshness throughout the year. Although an evergreen tree is throughout the Bible the symbol of the man of God, its flourishing appearance can be used equally well to symbolize the prosperity of the wicked; and so King David used the green bay tree in this wise: "I have seen the wicked in great power, and spreading himself like a green bay tree" (*Ps. 37:35*).

This tree is the *Laurus nobilis* of the botanists, and is

known to us as laurel. It should not be confused with
our native laurel, which is poisonous, and which belongs
botanically to the heath family. Through the ages, bay
leaves have been used as a condiment, and the berries,
leaves, roots and bark have long been employed in
medicine. The plants are decorative, having greenish-
yellow and succulent, purplish-black fruits which are
cherrylike in appearance.

Today, the sweet bay (*Laurus nobilis*) is the most
universal of tub plants, gracing the steps and terraces
of homes and public buildings, and decorating interiors
on special occasions. The head is usually kept trimmed,
often shaped as a pyramid, cone or globe, with the
body long or short to fit the formal garden or terrace
where it is to be placed. Plants may be cut back and
trimmed into shape once a year after the new growth is
well matured. The laurel is an excellent plant to use on
the steps or in the foyer of a church, since it can be
trimmed to harmonize with any style of architecture.

Laurel trees can stand several degrees of frost, and
thrive best in good, loamy soil with leaf mold. In spring
and early summer, when they are making and finishing
their growth, they need a large quantity of liquid
manure or a strong manure mulching, for they are great
feeders. They are propagated by cuttings and by seeds,
but the most successful way to have such a plant is to
buy a tubbed one from a nurseryman. The larger specimens are expensive, but small ones are available in
gallon tub size for half a dollar. The bay tree needs
plenty of fresh air and water if it is to be kept indoors
as a house plant. In mild regions it makes a good hedge
and can stand hard pruning.

HEATH

The word heath appears twice in the Bible, and is mentioned in both instances by Jeremiah. In one instance, he says: "Flee, save your lives, and be like the heath in the wilderness" (*48:6*). In the other instance, he compares the man who trusts in himself, rather than in God, to the "heath in the desert" (*17:6-8*).

Most authorities believe that heath is a mistranslation and that the plant which Jeremiah had in mind was the savin juniper (*Juniperus sabina* or *Sabina vulgaris*) or the common juniper (*Juniperus communis*). Both plants are common throughout deserts, plains and rocky places of the Holy Land.

The savin juniper is often found among high mountains and isolated rocks, inaccessible to all save the bounding gazelle, so that when Jeremiah says, "Flee, save your lives, and be like the heath in the wilderness," his figure of speech could have appropriately referred to the juniper which lived in inaccessible places. Not all Bible commentators are in agreement about this, however. Some translate the heath of this passage as guinea hens, goats, and wild asses, since they, too, lived among the rocky crags that were inaccessible to man.

The savin and common junipers have been introduced into this country and are now frequently seen. Hardy in the North, the dwarf forms are used for covering rocky slopes or sandy banks and for outdoor window boxes during winter. Junipers like open, sunny situations. They can be propagated by seeds which germinate in the second or third year, by cuttings of nearly ripened wood, and by layering. For the average gardener, nursery stock will be more satisfactory.

JUNIPER

The heath of the Bible is a juniper, but the juniper is the desert broom or retam or *Genista*.

It was under a juniper tree that Elijah stopped to rest and sleep after his flight from Jezreel and Jezebel. Elijah had destroyed the prophets of Baal, his God had broken the drought that had caused a famine, but Jezebel, a Baal worshiper, had threatened Elijah's life. After his flight into the wilderness, Elijah slept under a juniper bush. An angel of the Lord appeared to him there, and provided him with meat and drink so that he would be sustained during the forty days and forty nights he was to spend on Horeb, the mount of God.

The broom, prevalent in the rocky places and ravines of the Holy Land and the surrounding country, is known botanically as *Retama retam* or *Genista monosperma*. Its leaves are small and sparse, but it has many slender, grayish branches and forms a dense bush from ten to twelve feet high, providing a shade to be grateful for in desert places devoid of other vegetation.

A number of different species of *Genista* are grown in this country, including the Bible species, *monosperma*. They are not hardy in the North, being suited to the drier climates of the United States. They grow in any well drained soil and like a sunny position. Useful for covering dry, sandy banks and rocky slopes, they are also attractive in borders and rockeries. They are propagated by seeds sown in spring, also by layers and by greenwood cuttings under glass. The broom makes a beautiful shrub, and during the blooming season is covered with small, fragrant, pealike, white flowers.

JUNIPER ROOTS

In Job (*30:4*), we read that juniper roots were used for meat. The roots of the broom are nauseous, but upon the roots exists a fleshy parasite which grows about a foot tall, bearing crimson spikes of inconspicuous flowers. It is believed that these parasites were the juniper roots of this reference.

Coals of juniper are mentioned in Psalms (*120:4*). The roots of the broom are used in making charcoal.

MULBERRY

When the Philistines heard that David had been anointed king over all Israel, they immediately set out to make war upon him. David inquired of God, saying, "Shall I go up against the Philistines?" And God said, "Go up; for I will deliver them into thine hand."

David met and defeated them in battle, and burned their gods, but they rallied and spread themselves again in the valley ready for another encounter. This time when David inquired of God, he was told not to approach them directly but to turn away, and come upon them "over against the mulberry trees." When David heard the "sound of going in the tops of the mulberry trees," he fell upon the Philistines, for this was the signal that God had gone forth ahead of David to smite the enemy (*I Chron. 14:14-15*).

Modern students of the Bible believe that the word mulberry as it appears in this passage in the King James version is a mistake, and that the true translation should be aspen or trembling poplar. Ordinarily, a breeze stirring the leaves of mulberry trees would make no sound because the leaves are soft, but a breeze in the tops of aspens or poplars whose leaves are stiff, would have made sufficient sound to give David the awaited signal. *Populus euphratica* and *Populus tremula* have both been suggested as the trees of this passage, and both species are cultivated in this country.

We have our own native species of trembling aspen (*Populus tremuloides*), so similar to the *P. tremula* of Palestine that on the basis of appearance no one could challenge your choice of this native tree for the Bible garden; only the botanist would be able to tell them apart. The bark is whitish gray, making saplings conspicuously lovely in a thicket. The native aspen is generally distributed in North America—north of Pennsylvania and Kentucky, extending to Mexico in the mountains.

Trees of the poplar family are among the easiest of all trees to propagate and grow. They come readily from hardwood cuttings and thrive in almost any soil. They grow to a height of from fifty to sixty feet.

MYRTLE

When Isaiah made glowing predictions of future prosperity, he said that the myrtle tree would grow in the desert, and replace the briers. The myrtle, a handsome, bushy evergreen with fragrant flowers, was a symbol of divine generosity, an emblem of peace and joy. It was used along with the branches of other evergreen trees in religious ceremonials. The Hebrews gathered its boughs and brought them to shade their outdoor dwellings at the Feast of the Tabernacles, when they sat beneath their thick-leaved booths erected on the flat roofs of houses, and called on the widow, the orphan, and the stranger to put away their sorrow and rejoice in the Lord.

This habit had been forgotten during the sad days of exile, but was revived by Nehemiah. After their return from Babylon, the Jews became discouraged in the work of rebuilding their city, until Nehemiah, aristocrat and cup-bearer to King Artaxerxes, obtained permission to return to Jerusalem and direct the work. After the wall of the city was finished, he called forth Ezra, who read from the scroll containing the laws which the Lord had given Moses, in which the Children of Israel had been directed to gather the branches of myrtle and pine trees to make booths upon their roofs and in their courts and in the courts of the house of God and in the streets. And so they did this, and there "was very great gladness" (*Neh. 8:14-16*).

In good environments in Palestine the myrtle (*Myrtus communis*) grows to twenty or thirty feet tall, but is more often a small bush. Its wood is hard and mottled, often knotty, and is highly valued in turnery. The flowers, leaves and fruit of the myrtle have always been employed in making perfume, and are so used today.

In this country it is a handsome, bushy evergreen, growing to ten feet, with glossy, dark-green, scented leaves and fragrant flowers like white stars, followed by blue-black berries. It thrives in well drained loam soil with leafmold added, and likes an abundance of water in summer. It is propagated by cuttings of half-ripened shoots under glass and by layers. Valuable for hedge or screen planting in mild regions, the myrtle is a good pot or tub plant in colder regions, and is excellent for summer porches and terrace decorations in the north.

OAK

Oaks grew on hills and mountainsides in Palestine, in Bashan and Gilead east of Jordan, and in scattered groves on the slopes of the Maritime Plain. Isolated trees which grew to a large and massive size were scattered throughout the country; important covenants were often made under their branches, and the dead buried beneath their shade. There were many different species, but the evergreen oaks were most cherished by the people of the Bible lands because any tree which retained its leaves and remained green all year seemed proof of the everlasting goodness of the life that flowed from God. The evergreen habit of oaks and cedars, of myrtle, bay and olive was especially appreciated in a land that was so dry during part of the year that other vegetation almost completely disappeared.

The oak was respected and venerated; strong men were compared to its strength—the Hebrew word for oak was strong-tree. But it was also a pitfall in the path of the Hebrew who, sometimes, fell to worshipping the tree instead of the God who made it. Sacred groves and sacred oaks abounded in the land, having been held sacred by the worshipers of Baal. The words of the prophets are charged with scorn for those who worshiped trees in groves or in their own gardens. Isaiah warned the people that they would be ashamed of their desire for oaks, (*1:29*) and he described the fate of the wicked in terms of the "oak whose leaf fadeth, and as a garden that hath no water." (*Isa. 1:30*).

Oaks and cedars are frequently associated with mountains and hills to denote loftiness of spirit, but when this loftiness fails to recognize God, it shall be humbled. "The lofty looks of man shall be humbled . . . For the day of the Lord of hosts shall be upon every one that is proud and lofty . . . upon all the cedars of Lebanon that are high and lifted up, and upon all the oaks of Bashan . . . and the Lord alone shall be exalted in that day" (*Isa. 2:11-17*).

It was in terms of the humbling of a tree, that Nebuchadnezzar learned that his own proud spirit was to be brought low. The lofty and spreading tree of which he dreamed was, according to many scholars, an oak tree (*Dan. 4:8-27*).

An oak tree plays an incidental part in the life of King David and the death of his son Absalom, and recalls the tragic story. It was in the branches of an oak tree that the heavy hair of Absalom became entangled so that he was trapped and killed (*II Sam. 18:9-10*). When David is told of his son's death he utters the anguished cry which has rung through the ages: "O my son Absalom . . . would God I had died for thee. O Absalom, my son, my son!" (*II Sam. 18:33*).

The handsome Holly, or Holm Oak (*Quercus Ilex*), is widely cultivated in this country. An evergreen tree which grows to a height of sixty feet, it has a large, round-topped head and is hardy as far north as Washington, D. C. This oak is probably the most available to gardeners who wish to include the oak in a Bible planting, and it is a lovely tree to represent the Bible oaks. Among other species named as Bible oaks are *Quercus Aegilops, Q. coccifera* and *Q. lusitanica*. They are cultivated in this country, but are not always easy to get.

OIL TREE

The oil tree, or oleaster, was a common tree in Palestine, and is known to us as the wild olive or Russian olive. The tree yields an oil which is sometimes used as medication but never as food. The hard, fine-grained wood is well suited to carving, and is believed to be the olive wood which was used for doors, temple posts and figures of cherubim (*I Kings 6:23, 31-33*).

Isaiah mentioned the oil tree with the cedar and myrtle and others, when he spoke of the glorious day when the Lord alone would be recognized as God, when the dry places would be richly watered and the desert covered with glorious vegetation (*Isa. 41: 19, 20*).

This graceful shrub, with small, narrow, silvery leaves and inconspicuous flowers, is widely grown in our own country in the East and South, in the Middle West and the Far North, into Canada. The silvery hue of this species (*Elaeagnus angustifolius*) makes it a handsome ornamental. It grows to about twenty feet and is sometimes spiny. It grows in any well drained soil, including limestone, and prefers a sunny place. In many parts of the south it has escaped cultivation and become naturalized. Propagation is by cuttings of mature and half-ripened wood, by layers and root cuttings, and by seeds which germinate in the second year; they should be stratified and sown the second spring.

PINE

Pines grew in abundance with other conifers in the Bible Land, and so were mentioned along with other evergreens to illustrate the prosperity and beauty of life in the days when the Lord should be worshipped in all the land.

The Aleppo pine (*Pinus halepensis*) and the stone pine (*Pinus pinea*) were both common in Palestine, and are both frequently grown in the United States, although they are not hardy in the North. The Aleppo pine is very common in seaside planting and will thrive in almost any sandy or rocky, barren place where the climate is right. It grows sixty feet tall, with short branches and yellowish or brownish branchlets and light-green leaves. Its bark is gray and smooth, becoming fissured in age.

The green fir tree of Hosea (see section on fir) is believed to be the stone pine because of its edible fruit. This tree is one of picturesque habit with a trunk usually destitute of branches for a considerable height, and with a wide-spreading, parasol-like head.

POPLAR

Poplars are common in Palestine, particularly near watercourses, and in the Bible text they appear as poplars, mulberries, and willows. The white poplar (*Populus alba*) is the species of Hosea (*4:13*) : "They sacrifice upon the tops of mountains, and burn incense upon the hills, under oaks and poplars and elms, because the shadow thereof is good." Its young buds give off sweet, balsamic odor in spring; and, on being bruised, yield a fragrant, resinous substance.

The white poplar is a large, much-branched tree, growing to a height of ninety feet, with whitish bark on the young branches which become dark-colored and rough on the mature parts. Poplars are among the easiest of all trees to propagate and grow. They thrive in almost any soil. One variety of the white poplar (*nivea*) has escaped from cultivation and grows wild in many regions of the United States.

Under the section on mulberry, we have already mentioned the trembling aspen or *Populus tremula*.

SHITTAH TREE

Directions for building the Tabernacle and the Ark of the Covenant were given to Moses in the wilderness. Shittim wood from the shittah tree was specified in the building of both. The wooden structure of the Tabernacle was to be of shittim wood as were, also, the altar and table. The chest or ark was to be made of this wood overlaid with gold: "And thou shalt make staves of shittim wood, and overlay them with gold . . ." (*Exo. 25:13, 28*). The ark has great significance in the life of the people of the Old Testament, and since it occupied the most holy spot of the sanctuary, it tended to exclude any idol from the center of worship.

The identity of the shittah tree has caused no controversy whatsoever because everybody agrees that it is the acacia tree—the only timber tree of any size in the Arabian desert. It grows and thrives in dry situations where no other tree is able to grow. In favorable localities, the acacia may attain a considerable size, growing from twenty to twenty-five feet tall, but in the desert it is usually a bush with strong, white spines about one and one half inches long. Its blossoms are yellow and its fruit is a legume or pod. The wood used for clamps on mummy coffins in Egyptian tombs has been identified as shittim or acacia wood.

The acacia tree (*Acacia seyal and A. Tortilis*) did not grow in northern Palestine, but was common in the southern and drier parts of the country. The place-names Shittim, Valley of Shittim and Abel-Shittim, occur in the Bible, and meant "the meadow or moist place of the acacias."

Acacia wood is close grained and hard, orange brown in color, and much valued in cabinet work. Its bark is used for tanning leather. The present-day Arabs of the desert gather its wood and burn it for fuel, and collect its foliage and flowers to serve as food for their cattle.

Many people have confused the American black locust with the acacia of the Bible. The black locust (*Robinia pseudo-acacia*) thrives in the Holy Land today, but it has been introduced into the country since the discovery of America.

TAMARIX

The Hebrew word *eshel* has been translated as both grove and tree in several places in the Old Testament.

Examples are: "Abraham planted a grove in Beer-sheba (*Gen. 21:33*); ". . . under a tree in Ramah" (*I Sam. 22:6*); ". . . under a tree at Jadesh" (*I Sam. 31:13*). Most authorities are of the opinion that *eshel* in these verses should have been translated tamarix.

The tamarix tree was certainly a commonplace tree in the dry sections of Palestine during Bible times, and must surely have been in the minds of those who spoke of trees. Beer-sheba, where Abraham "planted a grove," was a region of great droughts which would have made the cultivation of any other trees almost impossible.

In the extreme southern portion of the desert of Shur —the scene where Hagar wandered with her outcast child—the stunted bushes of tamarix have been found in abundance in modern times, and some travelers have remarked that it was probably under such a tree that the despairing mother cast the child of her blighted hopes.

The tamarix or tamarisk thrives in sandy environments, remaining green when all the surrounding vegetation is dry and brown. Its showy panicles of pink or whitish flowers, and the fine, graceful foliage, make it an ornamental and popular tree for the garden. These trees will endure dry soil and saline conditions, thriving in seaside planting where they are dashed by salt spray. Some are fairly hardy as far north as Massachusetts. *Tamarix orientalis, T. pentanda, T. tetragyna* and *T. articulata* are given as the particular Bible species.

TEIL TREE

The teil tree of Isaiah (*6:13*) is the large and beautiful terebinth which grew on the rocky hillsides. It is

described in the section on elm, which is also believed
to be a terebinth, rather than a true elm.

WILLOWS

A number of true willows grew in Palestine, and
there are few places where one species or another may
not be found along the watercourses. Bible commentators believe, however, that poplars and oleanders as
well as willows were included in the verses where willows by the watercourses or willows by the brook are
mentioned.

The most famous willows of the Bible appear in one
of the best loved Psalms (*137:1-3*) :

By the rivers of Babylon,
There we sat down, yea, we wept,
When we remembered Zion.
We hanged our harps upon the willows in the midst thereof.
For there they that carried us away captive required of us a song;
And they that wasted us required of us mirth, saying,
Sing us one of the songs of Zion.

A legend grew up around these willows upon which
the exiles hung their harps. The story has it that the
harps weighted down the branches, so that they drooped
forever after. This legend about the weeping willows
reached Europe along with the tree. The botanists, ac-
cepting it as a native of Babylon, gave it the name *Salix
babylonica.* Years later, the weeping willow was discovered to be a native of China, a tree that had not
been introduced into Babylon during Old Testament
days. After further study, it was decided that the exiles
must have hung their harps upon the aspen (*Populus*

euphratica) which grew along the Babylon river banks. The leaves of this aspen hang downward although their drooping appearance is not so pronounced as that of the weeping willow.

Of the botanical species mentioned as the actual willows of the Bible—*Salix alba, acmophylla, fragilis* and *octandra*—two are common and even naturalized in this country. The white willow (*Salix alba*) grows to a height of seventy-five feet; the trunk is short and thick, the branches are yellowish brown and the leaves ashy gray and silky. It is often used to guard the banks of streams against erosion.

The brittle or crack willow (*Salix fragilis*) is very common in this country. It grows to a height of from fifty to sixty feet. A stake cut from the tree and driven in the ground will soon root and grow.

The oleander (*Nerium oleander*), included in some of the willow references by Bible authorities, forms extensive thickets in parts of the valley of the Jordan. Streams in the Holy Land are often lined with groves and thickets of its tall stems, thickly clustered with rose-like blossoms and dark, narrow, firm evergreen leaves. In the South in the United States the oleander grows outdoors. In the North it is grown as a tub plant outdoors in summer and stored in the cellar during the winter. Clippings will root easily in a bottle of water. This plant is poisonous, so leaves or flowers should not be put in the mouth.

4

A Garden of Herbs

AT THE opposite end of the vegetable kingdom from
the stately and magnificent cedar of Lebanon,
stands the lowly hyssop. It was said of Solomon, in
proof of his wisdom, that he could talk upon any subject
from the cedar tree that was in Lebanon even unto the
hyssop that springeth out of the wall (*I Kings 4:33*).

And this humble hyssop has stirred up more controversy than any other plant mentioned in the Bible; at
least, it has consumed more pages of discussion. Every
writer or reader familiar with hyssop literature will
tell you that Celsius, author of the *Hierobotanicon*—
foundation stone of Biblical botany—devoted forty-two
pages to the subject, and discussed eighteen kinds of
plants without arriving at a conclusion.

Is the Biblical hyssop, the marjoram, the caper plant,
the sorghum, the maidenhair spleenwort or the wall-
rue? It may have been any one of these, so say the
authorities, but it could never be the hyssop of our herb
gardens, the plant which Linnaeus called *Hyssopus officinalis*, native to southern Europe but not to the Holy
Land or to Egypt.

Plants that represent the hyssop will grow in our
modern gardens, as will also mint, cumin and rue, specifically mentioned by Jesus. Basil, lavender, pennyroyal,
horehound, thyme and rosemary are native to the Holy

Land, and as such may be included in a Biblical garden of herbs. We do not know that all herbs native to the Bible lands were cultivated, but we do know that some of them were, for only cultivated plants were subject to tithe; and Jesus said, "Ye pay tithe of mint and anise and cummin" (*Matt. 23:23*). And he also said: "For ye tithe mint and rue and all manner of herbs" (*Luke 11:42*).

The phrase, a garden of herbs, is used several times in the Bible; Egypt, where grew flavoring herbs, potherbs and vegetables, was so described. King Ahab demanding a vineyard from Naboth, said: "Give me thy vineyard, that I may have it for a garden of herbs" (*I Kings 21:2*). We know that every man of property had a garden because gardens of figs, olives and vines are frequently mentioned. Isaiah writes of "a garden of cucumbers," and so there were, no doubt, gardens of other vegetables and of kitchen herbs.

Modern herb gardeners claim as their own all plants used for flavoring—those known as spices and those of medicinal value—so that many Bible plants belong, in all fairness, to the herb garden. Besides the kitchen herbs, it is proper to plant the mustard seed of the parable of Jesus, the castor bean of Jonah's experience, the biblical flax, the bay tree whose leaves flavor soups and dressings, myrtle leaves popular in potpourris, and the aromatic plants of the chapter on perfumes. Garlic, leek and onions are classed sometimes as flavoring herbs, sometimes as vegetables. They are included in this chapter, as are cucumbers and watermelons.

The plants of your own Bible garden may be divided into flower, herb or vegetable gardens, but there is no

reason so to segregate the plants. Trial Bible gardens
have already combined in perfect harmony herbs, flowering plants, vegetables and grains. Since the word garden
was derived from the Persian word for paradise, even
the humblest garden can be identified with the great
garden in Genesis in which also grew plants "good for
food."

On the night of the Passover, the Israelites are described as eating bitter herbs with unleavened bread and
roasted lamb (*Exo. 12:8; Numb. 9:11*). A number of
commentators think that the bitter herbs of these passages refer not to mint, as many writers have supposed,
but to plants like lettuce, endive, young leaves of chic-
ory, dandelion, and sorrel, eaten as salad. It is reasona-
ble to suppose that these weedy and widely distributed
plants, common in Egypt and western Asia were the
bitter herbs of the Passover. At the present time, these
and similar plants are eaten by the Arabs. Many authorities translate bitter herbs specifically as endive, and
endive appears in ancient Greek Alexandrian translations.

ANISE

Jesus rebuked the Pharisees for putting more stress
on the outer than upon the inner duties of their religion.
In the King James version the verse reads: "Woe unto
you, scribes and Pharisees, hypocrites; for ye pay tithe
of mint and anise and cummin, and have omitted the
weightier matters of the law" (*Matt. 23:23*). The word
anise is considered a mistake in translation; most modern translators quote this passage as "mint and *dill* and
cummin."

Dill (*Anethum graveolens*) was prized in ancient days, as it is today, for its warm and stimulating properties. Today it is used in cookery and medicine, and is familiar to most of us as the dill of dill pickles. A member of the Parsley family, it is an annual or biennial, and easy to raise from seed. Sow in moist, sandy soil where the plants will receive plenty of sun, and where they are to grow, because the root system is too delicate for transplanting. Cultivate frequently.

Dill grows from two to three feet high, and needs staking. It has feathery leaves, and in midsummer bears flat terminal umbels with numerous yellow flowers. It makes an excellent house plant when in a pot, where it does not grow so tall as in the garden. The germinative quality of the seeds lasts for three years.

To harvest, cut the ripening heads in midsummer and spread thinly on a sheet. When dry, thresh with a light rod. Clean and store the seeds in cotton sacks in a dry place. Or, instead of threshing the seeds, gather the branches, bind in small bunches, and hang up to dry. Dill can be used in flavoring soups, in spicing beets and pickles, and in pastry.

CORIANDER

When the Children of Israel wandered in the desert and received manna for food, they described it as looking like coriander seed (*Exo. 16:31* and *Numb. 11:7*). Coriander grows wild all through the Holy Land, and was used by the ancients as a condiment and medicine.

Coriander (*Coriandrum sativum*) is an annual which grows from one and a half to two feet high. Another

member of the Parsley family, it is of easy cultivation
in any garden soil, but prefers a warm, dry, light one.
Seeds are sown in the autumn or early spring, the latter
time in the North. Do not transplant seedlings, for the
root system is too delicate. The seed heads, which ripen
about midsummer, are gathered and dried on sheets,
then beaten with light rods to separate the seeds. If
ripened seeds are not harvested promptly, the heavy
seed falls to the ground and re-seeds.

This plant is grown for its aromatic seeds, which are
used for flavoring pastries, sausages, candies, salads,
soups, puddings, curries, wines and even "hot dogs."

Plants can be potted and grown in a sunny window all
season.

CUCUMBER

These juicy, watery vegetables are always delicious
in any climate, and their refreshing coolness was particularly valued during the hot, dry season in Palestine
and Egypt. In Egypt, in the valley of the Nile, cucumbers grew luxuriantly and were eaten and enjoyed by
the Children of Israel.

When Moses led them out of Egypt and into the
Arabian desert, cucumbers and other vegetables were
no longer available. The fruits and vegetables, the fish
and fowl of their Egyptian days were but a memory.
Food in the desert was scarce; God sent them manna
every day so that there was bread, but they were dis-
contented with such a diet. They complained bitterly to
Moses: "We remember the fish, which we did eat in
Egypt freely; the cucumbers, and the melons, and the
leeks, and the onions, and the garlick: but now our soul

is dried away: there is nothing at all, besides this manna, before our eyes" (*Numb. 11:5, 6*). Why have you brought us to this evil place, they said, where there are no figs, grapes or pomegranates; there is no water here to drink, either! (*Numb. 20:5*). They had forgotten their unhappy days as bondsmen; now they longed for Egypt as a land in which there was plenty to eat.

The cucumbers for which they longed were of the same species which we grow in America today. This plant has been in cultivation since time immemorial, so long in fact that it is not known as a wild plant. Its wild ancestors and the country in which they first grew are lost in the mists of time.

Cucumbers were cultivated by the Hebrews in the Promised Land, and Isaiah makes specific reference to a garden of cucumbers (*Isa. 1:8*).

A cucumber vine (*Cucumis sativus*) will make satisfactory growth anywhere in the garden provided it is given an abundance of rotted manure. Cucumbers should be planted as early as possible, perhaps in April but they will not tolerate cold, wet soils or frosts. Plant in hills, a few seeds one inch deep in each hill, and protect the tender plants with a hotcap. These paper cones can be purchased from any gardening supply house. Continue to use the cap until the plant is sturdy enough to maintain itself, but the cap must be ventilated on warm days. The plants require from sixty to eighty days to mature.

Keep the crop picked; the vine will not continue to produce if the cucumbers are permitted to ripen upon it. They can be harvested at any stage of growth depending upon their purpose.

Cucumbers may be pickled, and are excellent products to sell at a church bazaar. Dill pickles combine the use of two Bible plants.

CUMIN

Isaiah, after rebuking Ephraim for her sins, closes his speech on a note of hope. His listeners must not feel that they are going to be punished to the point of extermination. God will not be too severe in His judgments and will not bruise His people needlessly. God will deal differently with different people, just as the farmer uses different, methods in threshing such crops as fitches, cumin, wheat and barley. Fitches are beaten out with a staff, cumin with a rod. Bread corn is threshed with a cart wheel, but it is never bruised by driving the wheel over it more than is necessary (*Isa. 28:24-29*). Isaiah, in using this illustration from agriculture, was talking in terms which every farmer of his day could easily understand.

Cumin—spelled with one "m" today, and botanically known as *Cuminum cyminum*—a member of the Parsley family, is an annual which grows about six inches high, and has clusters of small, white or rose flowers. Plants are easily raised from fresh seed sown in early spring in light, fertile soil in a warm, sunny, protected spot. Sow the seeds where they are to grow, since the root system is too delicate to permit transplanting. In harvesting, gather the umbels of seeds when ripe, that is, when brownish in color, and spread on a heavy cloth. Let them dry in a warm, airy room, then thresh the umbels gently so that the seeds are not bruised. The seeds are used as an ingredient in curry powder and for flavoring pickles, cheese, soup, pastry and chile con carne.

FLAX

Flax, the oldest known of textile fibers, was extensively cultivated in Egypt and Palestine in Bible days. By following the references to flax and linen in a Concordance, much of the background of the times can be visualized. Stalks of flax were laid on the flat roofs of houses, (*Josh. 2:6*), where they were dried and blanched in the sun. Spinning was woman's work (*Prov. 31:13, 19*), and the fine linens that were produced were used as hangings and curtains in the Tabernacle (*Exo. 26:31, 33*, and *35:25*), and in the coats, bonnets and linen breeches of the priests (*Exo. 39:27-29*).

Poor and rich alike wore linen garments, but fine linen was a mark of distinction, and kings and rich men were clothed in purple and fine linen (*Luke 16:19*). The sails of the ships of Tyre were made of fine linen from Egypt, and linen was part of the rich cargoes of the merchant ships (*Ezek. 27:7, 16*). Then as now, linen was used in home furnishings, for beds and curtains; a bed was made with fine Egyptian linen (*Prov. 7:16*), and in the description of the palace at Shushan (*Esther 1:6*) we read that cords of linen held the canopy over the garden court, where were white, green and blue hangings, fastened with cords of fine linen and purple to silver rings and pillars of marble.

Linen was used in burial, and the body of Jesus was wound in linen cloths with spices, as was the manner of the Jews in burial (*John 19:40*). Fine white linen

clothed the angels and was the bright and pure raiment
of the Lamb's wife (*Rev. 19:8*).

Flax (*Linum usitatissimum*) has long been a favorite
plant of the flower and herb garden. Its delicate blue,
or sometimes white, five-petaled flowers are attractive
in any planting. The extremely slender stems grow from
one to four feet tall and have numerous small, pale-
green, pointed leaves.

When planted in full sun, flax will bloom abundantly
until frost. Seeds may be sown indoors and set in the
garden, or sown where the plants are to stand. Flax has
escaped from gardens in many sections of the United
States and is frequently found beside railroad tracks
and in other uncultivated areas.

GARLIC, LEEK AND ONION

These vegetables, longed for by the Israelites in the
desert, have always been prized in the East as food.
They appear among the offerings to heathen gods, and
powers of magic were attributed to them. Garlic and
onions were among the favorite vegetables of kings,
also, for in those ancient days their strong odors were
not considered objectionable. Centuries later our sense
of smell became so refined that a breath redolent of
garlic and onions became offensive.

Garlic, leeks and onions are strong-scented plants of
the Lily family with white, yellow, rose or purplish
flowers. The garlic of the Bible is the common garlic
of our modern gardens, *Allium sativum*. No special
treatment is required but the plants like a rich, loamy
soil. The garlic plant seldom produces seeds, and is

propagated by planting the small cloves which make up the large bulbs. Separate them carefully, and when planting set about six inches apart. These perennials grow about twelve inches high, with very narrow leaves, and can be used as hardy border plants.

If the bulbs are to be used in the kitchen, then in autumn when the leaves have dried, the plants are dug, braided by their tops, and hung in any airy place to dry.

The leek, (*Allium porrum*) is a biennial, a stout plant which grows two feet or more in height, from a bulb that is milder in flavor than the onion. A light, rich, friable, moist but well drained soil is ideal, but any good garden loam will give satisfactory results.

The onion (*Allium cepa*) is our common onion, a hardy biennial herb. The most practical method of growing onions is to plant sets in the spring, after which the plants must be constantly cultivated. Modern observers say that the onion of Egypt is of marvelous sweetness, more delicious than the onions of our Occidental kitchens; and the shallot (*Allium ascalonicum*) is listed as one of the species which the Children of Israel longed for in the desert. This is a small, mild-flavored species of onion. Plant late in August or early in September. During winter, protect tops with a light covering of straw or other similar light material.

GOURD

The gourd of Jonah (*4:6*) is thought by some to have been the plant known to us as castor bean (*Ricinus communis*). This plant grows quickly and makes a delightful shade with its large, beautiful leaves.

Jonah had been called by the Lord to preach to the people of Nineveh. He was so successful in his preaching that the people repented of their wickedness and were forgiven by God. But Jonah's heart was hard against them; he wanted to see them destroyed. Jonah's attitude displeased the Lord, who decided to teach him a lesson. As Jonah stood in the hot sun looking down at Nineveh, a gourd or castor bean began to grow near him. It grew quickly and shaded Jonah from the heat. This made him very happy. He was so grateful for its cooling shade that he felt a sense of attachment for the plant, and when it died, he mourned its loss. A worm had cut its stem and deprived Jonah of the plant he loved.

If Jonah could become so attached to a plant which had sprung up in the night was it not to be expected that the Lord should have become even more attached to the people of Nineveh with whom He had had a long association? "And should not I spare Nineveh," the Lord said to Jonah, "that great city, wherein are more than sixscore thousand persons?" (*Jonah 4:11.*) And so Jonah learned a lesson in love and compassion.

The castor bean or castor-oil plant may be planted as a foliage specimen or a screen. It rarely reaches a height of more than twelve feet, but in the tropics it becomes a tree of forty feet. The leaves are large, sometimes three feet across. Young leaves are deep purple, old ones bright green. The flowers, without petals, are borne in panicles covered with dark brown spines; the fruit is a capsule containing three large seeds which yield the castor oil of commerce and which are recommended for ridding gardens of moles.

These plants are extremely easy to grow, and seeds may be sown in the garden or, if you live in the North, started under glass and transplanted to the garden in May. The soil may be clay or sandy loam but should have good drainage. The seeds are poisonous, and should not be put into the mouth.

HYSSOP

Three different localities are concerned in the references to hyssop—Egypt, the Desert of Sinai and Palestine; and so if the hyssop of the Bible is always to be the same plant, it must be a plant that grows in all three places. Since a number of different species of marjoram are native to all of these localities, marjoram has come to be favored by many authorities as the plant actually used in the hyssop references.

The first reference is in connection with the great deliverance from Egypt. Moses was to lead the Children of Israel out of Egypt, but Pharoah was loath to lose his good slaves. In order to make Pharaoh change his mind, Egypt was visited with plagues of frogs, lice, flies, hailstones and locusts. But Pharaoh was stubborn, and did not give in until the destroying angel claimed all the first-born in Egypt. The Israelite households were "passed over" on this dreadful night of doom, because each house had been marked with the blood of the lamb. Moses, in order that the first-born of his own people might be spared, had given these instructions: "And ye shall take a bunch of hyssop, and dip it in the blood that is in the bason (basin) and strike the lintel and the two side posts . . ." (*Ex. 12:22*).

This command came on short notice, so the students of biblical botany ask this question: "Which plant was available in such quantity that it could supply more than a hundred thousand families with brushes?" Marjoram and the caper could both have met the demand, say the champions of these plants. Other authorities hold that it was sorghum, not only because it was available in plenty, but because the Israelites were in the habit of using sorghum inflorescence spikes for brushes and brooms; therefore, it would have been natural to use them as brushes for sprinkling blood at this time of crisis.

In the desert, the Israelites received the laws of purification, and hyssop is mentioned in the ceremony of cleansing the leper. Marjoram and caper are put forth as the hyssop of this reference (*Lev. 14:4,6, 52*), and as both were available it is difficult to choose between them. Hyssop is mentioned in other books of Scripture, also, in connection with the cleansing of body and spirit. From Psalms (*51:7*) comes the familiar passage: "Purge me with hyssop, and I shall be clean: wash me, and I shall be whiter than snow."

In the New Testament a sponge filled with vinegar was placed upon a hyssop and raised to touch the lips of Jesus (*John 19:29*). In Matthew and Mark this instance is also mentioned, but the word reed appears instead of hyssop. The champions of sorghum put forth their choice here; they have a better case than the champions of caper, for the caper is inclined to spread itself as a vine rather than to hold its stems upright. Thus it would hardly have been long or rigid enough to be used as a stick. The chief claim for marjoram in this passage seems to rest upon the fact that the strong scent of the herb would have been refreshing to the suffering Savior.

So, like Celsius, most of the biblical botanists rest the case without coming to any definite conclusions; the safest thing to say is that several different plants must have been the hyssop of the Bible. For the Bible gardener today, the lack of a single choice is fortunate, since several attractive plants can be grown instead of one.

The caper (*Capparis spinosa*), a spiny shrub of straggling habit, reaches a height of three feet. It grows in profusion on hills around Jerusalem, in Egypt and in the desert. The flowers are large and white, beautifully set off by large stamens with purple filaments and yellow anthers. The plant may grow upright, but usually spreads itself weakly over the ground like a vine; it covers ruins and old walls like ivy. It may be grown in greenhouses in the North and outdoors in the warmer parts of the United States. Propagation is by seeds in the South, or by cuttings of ripe wood placed under a bell jar in the greenhouse. The flower buds, pickled, are sold as capers in the grocery store.

The Egyptian marjoram (*Origanum aegyptiacum*) is the species favored by botanists who believe that hyssop was marjoram, but this species is not ordinarily listed by seedsmen in this country. However, many species of *Origanum* were native to the region, and for our biblical gardens we might as well choose the marjoram that is nearest at hand and easiest to get. The seeds, which are very small, should be sown in a seed pan or flat, and the young plants shielded from strong sun until they are

growing well. The best results will come from buying
nursery stock. As a flavoring herb, marjoram is popular
for dressings and meat dishes; gather it for drying just
before it flowers.

Sorghum (*Holcus sorghum*) is a tall grass with broad,
coarse-textured leaves and large tassellike seed heads.
Sow the seeds in spring.

Maidenhair spleenwort (*Asplenium Trichomanes*) is
a popular fern grown both out of doors and in the greenhouse. This fern likes an abundance of moisture at the
roots, but will turn brown in the winter months in an
excessively moist atmosphere. It should be kept in a
lightly shaded position. Among the most pleasing of
rock-garden plants, maidenhair spleenwort requires well
drained soil, not too rich, but with plenty of lime, growing best in pockets between the stones. It is also a good
terrarium plant. The wall-rue (*Asplenium ruta-muraria*)
close kin to the maidenhair, is a delicate tufted species,
from two to four inches high, and grows on ledges in
our Northern States.

MALLOW

Job, reflecting on the misery of the outcast, says that
they had to "cut up mallows" for food (*Job 30:4*).
Most authorities are agreed that the plant referred to
was the saltwort (*Atriplex Halimus*), a saline plant
something like spinach and eaten by the poor in Palestine today, although it is a miserable diet. It is a strong
growing, bushy shrub five feet or more tall, with inconspicuous flowers and gray foliage, and cultivated in
California for hedges and for seaside planting.

MANDRAKE

The mandrake leads us back to the early days of Jacob, and the jealousy between his wives, Rachel and Leah. Rachel was the best loved, but barren; Leah had sons. Leah's son Reuben had been gathering mandrakes in the field, and Rachel asked that she might have them (*Gen. 30:14-16*). The Bible story tells us only of Rachel's request for the mandrakes; it does not say that Rachel believed in their magic qualities, although in those days the plant was held by the heathen to have magic powers.

The mandrake (*Mandragora officinarum*) is also known as the love-apple. It is a herbaceous perennial of the Nightshade family. From a large taproot, which is often forked, arise many lanceolate leaves about a foot long, lying flat on the ground in the form of a rosette. From the center of the rosette rise the flower stalks, each bearing a single, purple flower similar to that of the potato, and this flower is followed by a yellowish fruit. When perfect, the fruits lie in the center of the rosette of leaves like bird eggs in a nest. The plant is not often cultivated, but if obtainable, will grow readily enough.

MELON

The melons for which the Children of Israel longed in the desert were watermelons and muskmelons. The watermelon (*Citrullus vulgaris*) is a native of tropical Africa, and has been cultivated for centuries, reaching Egypt very early in history, so that it figures in Egyptian paintings.

The watermelon thrives best in warm, sandy soil that is well supplied with organic matter. It requires liberal moisture during early life and is a gross feeder.

Seeds may be started in pots, flats or frames about four weeks before they are to be planted outdoors. For the average small garden or for display purposes in a Bible garden, enough seed can be planted in one pot to furnish all the seedlings necessary for use; ten or twelve seeds can be planted in a six-inch pot. Seedlings should not be transplanted outdoors until the weather is absolutely settled.

The muskmelon (*Cucumis melo*) which we call cantaloupe can be grown wherever summers are long enough to permit melons to mature before frost.

MINT

The mint was mentioned in the verse from Matthew quoted in the section on anise, and is mentioned again in a similar verse in Luke (*11:42*).

Several mints are common in Palestine, and the botanists choose *Mentha sylvestris, M. longifolia* and *M. arvensis* as Bible mints.

Our common garden mint (*M. viridis*) is believed by many authorities to have been derived from the wild horsemint (*M. sylvestris*) since forms intermediate between garden and horsemint have been found. Garden mint is no longer known in the wild state.

Mints are perennials and grow easily in any good garden soil, preferably in a moist, sunny position. They tend to become established and run wild, and are easily propagated by cuttings, or by divisions, or in some cases by runners. They are very attractive planted around a sundial or pool, and make excellent house plants.

When harvesting, cut after the dew has disappeared, and before the hot sun has taken any oil from the leaves. Tie the stems loosely in bunches and hang to dry on strings in an airy room or attic. Bunches intended for sale at the church bazaar should be nearly equal in length and uniform in size to facilitate packing. When dry, place in air-tight boxes to prevent re-absorption of moisture.

MUSTARD

In the germination of a seed, Jesus recognized the work of the Heavenly Father. The Kingdom of God is compared to a mustard seed, one of the smallest of all seeds which, cast into the garden, grows into a tree that shelters the birds seeking rest.

Most commentators agree that the mustard to which Jesus referred was the ordinary black mustard (*Brassica nigra*) which must have been cultivated in those times. It must also have grown wild as it does in Palestine today.

This mustard does not usually grow more than three or four feet tall, although plants have been found that were ten or fifteen feet tall, with a main stem as thick as a man's arm. They are annuals, but in the fall their stems and branches become stiff and hard and of sufficient strength to hold small birds.

Although this parable of Jesus seems very simple, one could spend a lifetime trying to fathom the miracle of the germination of a seed, and indeed, these words of Jesus have been pondered through the centuries. The usual interpretation is that the gospel, once planted, will grow and fill the earth. But every gardener who watches the miracle of the sprouting seed and the plant it becomes will reflect anew upon this simple passage.

RUE

Rue (*Ruta graveolens*), one of the plants mentioned by Jesus in his rebuke of the Pharisees, is a perennial, shrubby plant, one of the old, pungent medicinal plants. It makes a beautiful edging for garden or walk and is a fine house plant. It prefers a soil with some lime, grows from two to three feet high, and bears yellow flower heads from June to August. It is propagated by seeds or by division in the spring.

WILD GOURD

In II Kings (*4:39-41,*), we read of the pottage eaten by Elisha and the sons of the prophets. Herbs and wild gourds had been shredded into the pottage, but when the men began to eat, they cried out: "O thou man of God, there is death in the pot."

It is fairly well agreed that the wild gourd was the poisonous colocynth (*Citrullus colocynthis*), close relative of the watermelon. This wild vine, which trails on the ground or climbs by means of tendrils, looks inviting and green when almost all other vegetation has withered in the drought. Known as the bitter apple, it is the source of the drug, colocynth, used in medicine. The fruit is about the size and color of an orange, has a smooth, hard rind when dry, and contains an intensely

Jonah's gourd is known to us as the castor bean.

The "lilies of the field" are known to us as poppy-flowered anemones.

bitter, soft, spongy pulp, which is a drastic cathartic. The fruit is very tempting to those unacquainted with its nature. It is sometimes cultivated in this country as a curiosity, or in collections of economic plants.

Sometimes these gourds are referred to as gall: "They gave me also gall for my meat" (*Ps. 69:21*).

WORMWOOD

The phrase wormwood and gall is a figurative expression used many times in the Bible to imply sore punishment or bitter suffering.

The wormwood which gave rise to the expression is believed to belong to that group of plants still known as wormwood, with whose botanical name *Artemisia* we are familiar. There are many species of *Artemisia*, some native to our own continent, but the Bible species are believed to be *Artemisia judaica*, *A. arborescens*, or *A. absinthium* which is the common wormwood of our herb gardens. Although not all authorities are agreed that this species is native to the Holy Land, it represents the type, and may well take its place in our Bible gardens.

5

Flowers of the Field

JESUS stood on the hillside surrounded by fields that
were bright with many wildflowers. He was talking
to the people about the importance of seeking the kingdom of heaven and the uselessness of devoting their
lives to worldly anxieties. Aware of the flowers blooming at his feet, he found in them a simple and beautiful
illustration of the truth that he was trying to teach:

"Consider the lilies of the field, how they grow; they
toil not, neither do they spin: and yet I say unto you,
that even Solomon in all his glory was not arrayed like
one of these. Wherefore, if God so clothe the grass of
the field, which to day is, and to morrow is cast into
the oven, shall he not much more clothe you, O ye of
little faith?" (*Matt. 6:28-30*).

The spiritual beauty that shines through this verse
has been precious to the hearts of men for almost two
thousand years. It matters little what type of flower
Jesus referred to as far as the spirit of the message is
concerned, but the botanists say that the lilies were the
gay colored anemones. The botanists have given us a
glowing scene upon which our inner eye may dwell, for
Palestine was, above all else, a land of wildflowers.
When the rain of heaven blessed the earth, the hidden
seeds and bulbs that lay dormant during the season of
drought began to grow. The land was soon aflame with

the brilliance of flowers whose names today were un-
heard of in Bible times—tulips, hyacinths, irises, cycla-
mens, morning-glories, pinks, scabiosas, geraniums, lupines, fritillaries, violets—and above all—anemones.

The poppy-flowered anemones grew everywhere.
Their tuberous roots, storage houses for food supplies,
rested in the parched ground during the dry season.
They were shriveled, hard as rocks, and dead looking,
but when the rains came, they stirred and wakened, and
burst into bloom. Their petals of purple, crimson and
gold were of such royal colors that not even Solomon,
in all his glory, could be arrayed like one of these!

The poppy-flowered anemone is accepted by most
Bible authorities as *the* lily of the field, although they
believe that Jesus referred, in general, to all of the
flowers that were blooming in the field about him.

Why, then, did the white Madonna lily become so
popularly associated with this verse in the minds of the
people of the Western world? The answer probably
lies in the fact that the Madonna lily was painted into
many pictures of the Madonna and Child, in scenes of
the Annunciation and of other events in the life of Christ.
But we must remember that these paintings were made
long after the time of Christ, and in Europe, by painters
who were not familiar with the Holy Land. The
Madonna lily (*Lilium candidum*) is present in Palestine today, however, although it is not common, but
the consensus of opinion is that it was introduced after
the time of Christ.

In Solomon's garden grew lilies also. The maiden
sings, "I am . . . the lily of the valley" (*Sol. 2:1*). The
beloved's lips are like lilies (*5:13*). Such phrases as

"to gather lilies" (6:2) and to "feed among the lilies," (6:3) are used. Almost everyone agrees that the Scarlet Turk's Cap Lily was surely among the lilies of Solomon's garden, although some translators contend that the lily of Solomon was the hyacinth, some believe it was the Sternbergia, and others that it was the jonquil, a species of narcissus.

The rose, next to the lily, is the most famous flower of the Bible. Its name, likewise, is believed to have been applied to a number of plants which blossomed on the land after the rains. In the Song of Solomon, the maiden sings "I am the rose of Sharon." The fertile plain of Sharon is near the seacoast, and, when the rainy season sets in, it is carpeted with fields of bright flowers, among which the narcissus, tulip, crocus and anemone are perhaps the most conspicuous. The word rose comes from a Hebrew word whose root means bulblike so that the name, rose, probably once applied to any flower with a bulbous root. Some authorities have chosen the narcissus and the red tulip as the rose of Sharon and as the rose of Isaiah's passage, "the desert shall blossom as the rose." Others identify the rose of Sharon with the rockrose, and the oleander. There are a number of native roses in Palestine, but few authorities believe that they were referred to specifically because they do not have bulbous roots, although they certainly must have been included in the verses which refer to the flowers of the field.

The people of Bible days probably referred to all flowers as lilies, roses or just flowers. This is true even today when so much more is known about different kinds and types of flowers and plants. In America, few of us call the flowers of the field by specific names; they are just wildflowers. Except for the most common wildflowers of our own immediate neighborhoods, few of us can name or identify many of them. If this is so with us, think of how much more true it was of Bible people, who lived in a land where the wealth of different kinds of flowers is so great that not even the modern botanists can begin to call them all by name. More than three thousand five hundred species are listed in the scientific books on the flora of the land—a remarkable number to be included in so small a country.

The flowers of the field or of the grass was a common phrase in Bible days, and appears in the Scriptures a number of times as a symbol of the evanescent beauty and frailty of human life. Job says that man born of woman is of few days, and full of trouble: "He cometh forth like a flower, and is cut down" (*Job 14:1, 2*). The Psalmist warns that man's days are as grass: "as a flower of the field, so he flourisheth. For the wind passeth over it, and it is gone; and the place thereof shall know it no more" (*Ps. 103:15, 16*). James used the same simile, in the New Testament, to urge humility: "Let the brother of low degree rejoice in that he is exalted: but the rich, in that he is made low: because as the flower of the grass he shall pass away" (*Jas. 1:9, 10*). Isaiah achieves an effective contrast between the impermanence of the flower, and the eternal value of God's word: "All flesh is grass, and all the goodliness thereof is as the flower of the field . . . the grass withereth, the flower fadeth: but the word of our God shall stand for ever" (*Isa. 40:6, 8*).

The contrast between the season of flowers and the

dry season of desolation colored the speech of the
Bible people, and although the blossoms of the desert
and of the rocky hills represented the transience of
human life, they themselves have remained immortal
in the word of God which, as Isaiah said, "shall stand
for ever." Their images lie pressed between the pages
of our Bibles; in our daily speech the flowers of the
field still flourish; and in our gardens they bloom again,
in their season.

Many of the flowers of the field of Palestine are kin
to the flowers of our gardens, but are only wild cousins
that have never been tamed. Others are the direct ancestors of our cultivated varieties, having traveled from
Asia to western Europe where they sometimes were
much transformed in the hands of the horticulturists,
so that we have varieties that are more adapted to living in the conditions of our modern gardens.

ANEMONE

There are a number of different varieties of the
Bible anemone (*Anemone coronaria*), which blossom
for us in gardens and in pots, forced for winter bloom.
The Bride and St. Brigid are well known varieties.
In the outdoor garden, they are useful in the border or
planted in clumps along the front edge of the bed, where
their bright green, deeply cut, parsley-like foliage is an
attractive background for the large, single and double,
many colored flowers which grow on stems that are
from six to eighteen inches high. In mild climates, the
tubers can be planted in August for bloom in late September and, according to the experience of many garden-

ers, for bloom all through the winter. In cold climates, the tubers are best planted in March for bloom in late April and May, or if planted in the fall, they should be given a heavy mulch during the winter.

Before planting, soak the hard, dry tubers in lukewarm water for about twenty-four hours. Plant in well drained, loamy soil, with the pointed tip not more than four inches under the surface; one and one half to two inches deep is enough, and from four to six inches apart. Tubers multiply annually, and seeds are easy to grow. Gather seeds from your plants when fully ripe and sow in June in a well sheltered bed, where the soil has been thoroughly pulverized. Sow seeds thinly and cover with about one quarter of an inch of rich, sandy soil. The young plants should receive plenty of sunshine, and should be kept moist. Transplant into beds in September or in spring, according to your climate. In cold regions, the bed of young plants will have to be kept heavily mulched in winter.

In a cold or a mild climate, anemones should be lifted from the ground each year for a rest of perhaps two months. They may be stored during this time in peat moss or in dry sand. In mild climates where it is possible to have a long season of bloom, it is wise to plant two separate crops, so that the tubers can rest at different intervals.

For indoor bloom, anemones can be forced for any time of year, depending on the planting. Tubers placed in pots in September or October should bloom during mid-winter. They should be kept well drained and not too wet or too warm before growth is well started; at flowering time they should have plenty of moisture.

Anemones, as cut flowers, are available from florists' shops during the winter months, so that between your own garden supply and the florist supply, the lilies of the field are available all year round as table decorations for any church gathering. Anemones, as cut flowers, must have fresh water in the vase each day.

BEDSTRAW

The yellow bedstraw (*Galium verum*) which grew in the Holy Land as one of the "flowers of the field" grows in our American gardens, and is often called Ladies' Bedstraw because a legend has it that this plant was one of those among the hay on which the mother of Christ rested in the stable. Today it grows in our herb gardens, in rockeries and on banks. It is a perennial with stems from one to three feet high, and is so much at home in our Eastern States that it grows wild in the fields.

CROCUS

The saffron of Solomon's garden is known to us today as the saffron crocus (*Crocus sativus*). It is the commonest, fall-blooming species. The stigmas of this plant supply the saffron of commerce. It has been cultivated from time immemorial, but it also grew wild in the fields of Palestine, as did many other species of crocus. It thrives in any well drained, sandy soil. The bulbs should be planted about three or four inches deep in a soil that has been worked thoroughly, and is free from clay or decaying manure of any kind. They should be placed only two or three inches apart if mass effects are desired, and planted in the spring for autumn bloom. This crocus is easily grown from seed, which will produce plants that flower in the third year. Seeds should be exposed to freezing before the natural germinating time.

CORNISH HEATH

Cornish heath (*Erica vagans*) is hardy in the New York region and in central New England. The plant grows to a height of one foot or a little more, and has needlelike leaves and flowers that are sometimes white, pink, or pale, purplish red. It requires a soil free of lime and thrives where there is plenty of leaf mold or peat.

CYCLAMEN

Several species of cyclamen grew wild all through the Holy Land, their cormlike tubers resting in the dry soil until the rains came and called them into bloom. The cyclamen pot plants (*Cyclamen indicum*) which are available in the florists' shops today, or which can be grown in greenhouses, are much more impressive than their wild kinsmen of the Palestinian fields, but they may well represent them since seeds and tubers of the original species are not available to us. They are exotic-looking plants with their fragrant, pink, purple or white, nodding flowers and their attractive foliage. They may be grown from seed sown in April or September in soil containing a large amount of sand and leaf mold. If they are sown in September, they should be wintered in a cool house. In May, transplant them to larger pots and place them in a shaded frame. By July, they will be large enough for flowering pots, which should be five or six inch ones. Bring them into the house before danger of frost, and keep them in a cool location until they have finished flowering. While in flower, they do best in a temperature of 55°. After flowering, they need a short rest but should not be allowed to dry out or else the bulb or tuber will be injured. When they start growing again, shake off the old soil and repot into smaller pots. Not more than half the tuber should be under the soil.

Tubers or young plants, that bloom the first year, may be bought at moderate prices. Unless facilities for growing seedlings for a year are available, tubers or plants will give more satisfactory results. The soil best suited for their needs is one containing two parts leaf mold, one part sand and one part loam.

FLOWER-OF-AN-HOUR

The flower-of-an-hour is the common name for *Hibiscus Trionum,* a half hardy, annual species of rose-mallow which bears yellow or white, dark-centered flowers, one to three inches across. They open wide in sunshine but close in shadow. The stems are about two feet high, but the plant is bushy and spreading; the main branches seldom remain upright, usually lying prostrate on the ground, and are particularly popular for rock work. This plant blooms profusely in hot weather and thrives in any open, warm situation. Seeds should be sown where plants are to stand. Flower-of-an-hour is also known as Bladder Ketmia and Trailing Hollyhock.

HERB ROBERT

This old-fashioned annual geranium grows to a height of nine or ten inches, and is also called red robin because of its small, bright-crimson flowers which bloom from June until October. It is excellent for the rockery because it spreads and covers the ground in a few seasons; it needs moist soil and some shade. It grows easily from seed, and reseeds itself.

HYACINTH

The hyacinth, mentioned by some translators as one of the lilies of Solomon's garden, was certainly one of the flowers of the field in Palestine. The wild hyacinth (*Hyacinthus orientalis*) grew everywhere, and even in ancient times had come under cultivation. When it traveled to Europe in the early sixteenth century, it was already highly developed. Even in those days it was a plant of both single and double varieties, with flowers of blue, bluish purple and bluish white. Other colors have arisen since then—red, yellow, and varying shades of lilac and purple. The bulb was taken to Holland, where it was grown in quantity to supply the rest of the world, and became known as a Dutch bulb.

Leaves are from eight to twelve inches long, and the flowers come in April and May.

Bulbs should be planted six inches deep (to the bot-

tom of the bulb) in well drained soil. It must be rich,
if the plants are to produce flowers of good size. The
ground should be carefully spaded to a depth of twenty
inches, so that the roots can push through it easily to
their full length of twelve or sixteen inches. Their root
growth is made in autumn, which is the time for planting them. They are handsome border plants, thriving in
full sun or partial shade, and need not be lifted until
they become crowded.

They are excellent plants for the indoor Bible plant
display or for decoration for a church gathering, since
they grow easily in pots. For growing indoors in pots,
large, solid bulbs should be chosen. A single bulb needs
a five-inch pot. Place a few pieces of broken pots or
other drainage material in the bottom of the pot, and
then fill with a rich, loamy leaf mold containing a lot of
sand. The pot should be filled lightly so that the bulb
can be pressed into the soil, leaving only the apex to
appear above the surface. Bury the pots to a depth
of eight or ten inches in the open ground or in a frame.
In about seven or eight weeks the roots are fully developed and the bulb has begun to sprout. When taken
indoors they should be kept in a subdued light and at
a temperature of about 50° until the sprout becomes a
vigorous green. The slower the forcing, the more lasting the bloom. Bulbs wanted for Christmas should be
put in pots by September. Some of the single hyacinths
may be grown in water. Special hyacinth bulb glasses are
obtainable from seed stores. They should be filled with
pure water, and the cup of the glass holds the bulb so
that its base just touches the water.

The glasses must be kept in a dark closet or cellar

until sufficient root growth is made and the main flower shoot is about three inches tall. This will take from eight to ten weeks. Gradually bring them into the light, and keep them in an airy, sunny location. Add water as it is required; a small piece of charcoal placed in the glass will keep the water pure and sweet.

ICE PLANT

The ice plant or fig marigold is listed botanically under the names of *Cryophytum crystallinum* or *Mesembryanthemum crystallinum*. It is a common house plant, popular in window gardens, and in hanging baskets. Its leaves are flat, fleshy and glistening; flowers small, whitish or light rose opening in the sun. It is sometimes used as a pot herb. In any situation it must be given good drainage; a light, sandy loam, mixed with brick rubbish broken small, is satisfactory. It can be propagated by seeds or cuttings. Cuttings should be dried in the sun for two or three days before they are inserted into the sand.

JONQUIL

The jonquil (*Narcissus jonquilla*) is a hardy species of narcissus, and is of ancient cultivation. Some authorities believe it to have been one of the lilies of Solomon's garden. It is a slender, graceful plant with glossy, dark green leaves, narrow and rushlike. Plants grow to a height of from one to one and a half feet, and each plant bears from two to six flowers. The deliciously fragrant flowers are popular in gardens, and also as cut flowers. They require little or no care. The trumpet-shaped flowers are rich yellow in color and come in close clusters.

LARKSPUR

Larkspurs (*Delphinium Ajacis*) bloomed in the fields of Palestine, and since Bible days have become favorite garden flowers of the Western world. Their handsome flower spikes of blue, violet and white and their stately stems of foliage make the garden beautiful all summer, from May until the last of August. They will thrive in any average garden soil, but for best results they should be planted in a rich, sandy loam exposed to sun. Deep preparation of the soil is important. These plants are annuals which grow about eighteen inches high; they are propagated by seeds, although the seeds are slow to germinate. Where the climate is not too cold, it is best to sow seeds in the fall. Plants grown from seed sown in the fall should bloom in May. Sow additional seed in the spring for later bloom. Where seeds cannot be sown in the fall, sow indoors in the spring and then transplant to the garden as soon as the weather is settled.

These flowers are excellent for cutting because of their lasting quality, and they are effective in flower arrangements.

LILY

The chalcedonicum or Scarlet Turk's Cap Lily, is one of the lilies of Solomon's garden. It is also known as Lily of Greece and Red Lily of Constantinople. An illustration of it appears on a vase which is believed to date from 2300 B.C.

The stem of this plant grows to a height of from two to four feet and is green with a tinge of purple and covered with white down; each plant has about a hundred leaves, the lower ones being horizontal and from two to six inches long, the upper ones are smaller and more erect. Three to six flowers of brilliant vermilion, sometimes dotted with purple with scarlet anthers are produced by each plant in July or early August. This *Lilium chalcedonicum* is easily grown in a sunny position, in a heavy, but well drained soil, even a little limy. It deserves wider popularity than it has received because of its distinct form and rich color. The bulbs should be planted about four inches deep. The seeds should be planted in fall. Bulbs should not be transplanted until in later years when they show signs of becoming crowded. Lilies look best when planted in bold clumps, rather than singly. A background of greenery enhances their charms.

LOOSESTRIFE

The purple or swamp loosestrife, (*Lythrum Salicaria*), also called Spiked Loosestrife and Black Blood, is native to the Holy Land, but is now so common in the United States that it is pictured in most of the books showing the wildflowers of the Eastern States. It grows in masses on low, marshy land and makes beautiful splashes of color in our American landscape. It is useful for planting about borders of ponds, and in low, wet places. It is of easy culture in any moist soil; planted amid shrubbery it is able to hold its own. It is propagated by division. Loosestrife grows to a height of two or three feet in the wild, but under cultivation will grow to a height of five or more feet, producing flowers in profusion all summer. The flowers are usually purple, but the variety known as *Lythrum roseum superbum* has especially large, rose-colored flowers, is taller and more robust, and blooms well into September.

LUPINE

A number of species of lupine are native to the shores of the Mediterranean, just as many are native to our own country. California is famous for its native lupines, and Texas also, where they are called bluebonnets.

Several species, native to Palestine, have traveled to Europe and to America where they are used in flower gardens, as fodder for animals, and as plants to be plowed under in order to enrich the soil. The lupine, listed as *Lupinus angustifolius,* is widely grown in Europe. It is an annual, one foot high, hairy, with dark blue flowers appearing in early summer.

Blue lupine (*L. hirsutus*) is an annual which grows from two to three feet high, has hairy stems branching toward the top; its blue flowers appear in July and August. It also is used ornamentally and as an economic plant. Various varieties of this species are advertised by nurserymen.

Yellow lupine (*L. luteus*) grows to a height of two feet; its yellow flowers appear in June and July, and are delightfully fragrant. It succeeds in the poorest soil and is useful not only as an economic plant to improve sandy soils but as a garden plant as well.

Lupines are propagated by seeds sown where the plants are to stand, as they do not bear transplanting.

MALLOW

The mallow (*Malva sylvestris*) is a biennial which sometimes is grown as an annual. Under some conditions, it becomes a perennial and is very useful in ornamental planting. It grows to a height of two or three feet, is rough and hairy, with branching leaves that are sharply lobed; the large flowers are sometimes purple, sometimes rose, and they grow wild along the waysides of America. They are of easy cultivation in the garden or border. Sow the seeds where the plants are to stand.

Although mallow is native to the Holy Land, it is not the mallow of Job. The Bible authorities, in tracing down the reference to the plant mentioned in Job, have decided that he referred to a plant known to us today as saltwort (*Atriplex Halimus*).

MARSH-MALLOW

This mallow (*Althea officinalis*) grows to a height of from three to four feet, is downy, with leaves that are sometimes heart shaped or three lobed. The flowers, which are an inch across, are blush or rose, and are clustered in the axils of the leaves. It is perennial in marshes, and has become an American wildflower. It is of easy cultivation in a moist spot in the garden, and is a close kin of the hollyhock, which comes from China.

MEADOW SAFFRON

The meadow saffron (*Colchicum autumnale*) is often called an autumn crocus. This colchicum and many other species were among the most prominent flowers of the field in the Holy Land. It is a low flowering bulb that blooms in August and September after its foliage has died down. The rosy purple or white flowers are about four inches tall. Bulbs planted in September flower within a few weeks. The following spring the leaves appear and die down again in early June. Mark the spot where they are planted so that you will not disturb them while the bulbs are dormant, for there is no growth above ground to warn you where they are. They need full sun, a well drained soil, and look best planted with other low growing plants since they bloom when they have no leaves. They can be grown in rockgardens, in beds or in grass, which is not too thick nor cut too often. They are effective when planted where the thyme creeps, and although thyme is not mentioned specifically as an herb of the Bible, it also was one of the flowers of the field, for many species grew in the Bible lands, even in the deserts. The meadow saffron is most effective when planted in masses, and will remain in good condition for many years. The plants should not be disturbed unless the flowers deteriorate, then they should be lifted and separated when the leaves die. It is often advertised as a bulb that will grow without soil or water because the bulb will bloom in the house without either.

NARCISSUS

The bunch-flowered, white narcissus was a wildflower of Palestine, and many authorities believe it is the rose of the Bible. This polyanthus narcissus, known to botanists as *Narcissus tazetta,* is the original type from which many garden forms of clustered narcissi have come. It is a species native to many different countries, and very variable in form.

Today, we grow a number of varieties in America, some in the outdoor garden, while others are used for forcing indoors. The flowers are usually from four to eight to a stem, have light yellow crowns, and are fragrant.

Outdoor varieties can be planted early in autumn in mild climates where they can make a good root growth before winter. They can be left in the ground for four or five years without disturbing.

For forcing narcissus bulbs indoors, put them in a bowl of water, propping them up with stones. The roots cling to the stones and thus anchor the plants.

NIGELLA

The garden plants which we call Love-in-a-Mist, Devil-in-a-Bush, and Fennel-Flower came from the Nigellas of the Holy Land, and the Fennel-Flower (*Nigella sativa*) was cultivated particularly for its black seeds, which are often called black cumin. Isaiah called them "fitches" in his parable about agriculture.

Nigella stems are erect and grow from one to two feet high; the leaves are finely divided and bright green. The flowers are showy white, blue or yellow, and look like radiant stars enveloped in a green mist of their own leaves. They bloom from June until September. They can be sown in fall or spring in the open border, but seldom do well if transplanted. By planting at different seasons, the bloom can be continued throughout the summer. They require little care, and thrive under almost any conditions.

PEONY

From the wild peony (*Paeonia officinalis*) of Palestine has come a number of peony varieties and hybrids which are grown in our modern gardens.

Peonies should be planted in September or October and placed where they will have plenty of light and air. The ground must be prepared carefully to receive them, if they are to give satisfactory bloom. Dig a hole about two feet across and two feet deep and fill with at least six inches of soil which contains a rich amount of plant food, and on top of this put any average garden soil with a good mixture of fine loam and leaf mold. When you plant peonies in this well prepared soil, set the roots so that the eyes or buds on the crown are two to three inches below the surface, with the roots going straight down. Roots must not come into contact with the plant food which has been put in the bottom of the hole; they will grow down to it in a year or two. They should not be planted in a low spot where water will stand on them. An annual top-dressing, put on plants in November and forked into the earth the next spring, should keep the plants in good condition. Liquid manure, applied in the growing season and at a time when the ground is dry, gives good returns. A liberal supply of water is necessary at all times and especially while in bloom.

Peonies bloom in May and June, and the plants stand severe cold as far north as Duluth, Minnesota, without any ground covering. Peonies are the most hardy, showy, and easily grown of all garden flowers. They live and thrive in the same spot for twenty and thirty years at a time.

PERSIAN AND TURBAN RANUNCULUS

These Persian buttercups (*Ranunculus asiaticus*) are very showy, coming in all brilliant colors, except blue, with double flowers, sometimes measuring two inches across. The fleshy roots, which resemble small dahlia tubers, are sold as bulbs. In the north where they are not hardy, they should be planted when frost is out of the ground in spring, about two inches deep and six inches apart. Make the soil very sandy on top so that the leaves will push through it readily without heaving the soil. They like plenty of moisture at the roots during the growing season. A well grown mass of these flowers is beautiful. They blossom about the last week of May and the first of June. The tubers should be lifted after the foliage has ripened, and stored in a cellar where they will not freeze until the following spring.

PHEASANT'S-EYE

The flowers known as pheasant's-eye and summer or autumn Adonis are very common in the Holy Land, and are also great favorites with American gardeners. The summer Adonis (*Adonis aestivalis*) is crimson with yellow centers, and the autumn Adonis (*A. annua*) is crimson with dark centers.

They thrive in light, moist earth, in sun or partial shade. These annuals are propagated by seed, which are slow-germinating; the fresh seed is sown in autumn or early spring.

ROSE

Although roses grew in Palestine, they do not seem to be mentioned by any word which refers specifically to them. We have noticed, already, that the word which has been translated rose refers to bulb. Roses must certainly have been included in the phrase flowers of the field however. The Dogrose (*Rosa canina*), the Phoenician rose (*R. phoenicia*), the Austrian Brier rose (*Rosa foetida*), and the Damask rose (*R. damascena*), were all present in Palestine and helped to make it a brilliant land of blossoms. The Damask rose is much cultivated today as a source of attar of roses for perfumery.

SALVIA

The common sage (*Salvia officinalis*) has been raised in herb gardens for centuries, and grows wild in all the

Mediterranean regions. It is grown commercially for its leaves which are used in seasoning and in medicine. It is a hardy, white, woolly plant which grows from six to twelve inches high. In early summer the upper parts of the stem bear blue, though sometimes pink or white, flowers.

Sage likes plenty of sun, and a rich, well drained, loamy soil. Divide the clumps biennially to keep them from becoming straggly. Propagated by seeds, cuttings, layering or division. The vitality of the seeds lasts for three years.

A species of salvia which is not cultivated in this country, but which would grow readily if seeds were available, is *S. judaica*. This plant furnished the inspiration for the design for the seven-branched candlestick which was used in the Tabernacle. The inflorescence of this plant has almost exactly the shape and form of the seven-branched candlestick, with its central spike and three pairs of lateral branches, bending upward and inward in symmetrical fashion. On each branch of the plant are whorls of buds, which, again, gave the idea to the artist for the "knops" or "knobs" on the Biblical golden candlestick.

The description of the candlestick appears in Exodus (*37:17-18*): "And he made the candlestick of pure gold: of beaten work made he the candlestick; his shaft, and his branch, his bowls, his knops, and his flowers, were of the same: and six branches going out of the sides thereof; three branches of the candlestick out of the one side thereof, and three branches of the candlestick out of the other side thereof."

STAR OF BETHLEHEM

The star of Bethlehem (*Ornithogalum umbellatum*) of our gardens was called dove's dung in the Bible.

After the death of Solomon, there was degeneration in the Hebrew nation, due to internal conflict from within, and constant threats from without. Samaria was besieged by the king of Syria. "And there was a great famine . . . until an ass's head was sold for four score pieces of silver, and the fourth part of a cab of dove's dung for five pieces of silver" (*II Kings 6:24, 25*).

Today the plains and hillsides of Syria and Palestine are sheeted in spring with the white flowers of a species of star of Bethlehem, the bulbs of which are used as food and called "dove's dung" by the Arabs, a name in common use among them for vegetable substances.

These dwarf, hardy bulbous plants bloom in May and June, the umbels of green and white flowers are brilliant: each flower is a pretty six-pointed star, opening in sunshine. The leaves are from six to twelve inches long, narrow, deeply channeled, and distinctly striped with white. They are excellent for the border, for outdoor window boxes, because the bulbs are hardy, and for gardening in uncultivated spots, because they spread readily.

STERNBERGIA

Many authorities believe that Sternbergia (*Sternbergia lutea*) was one of the lilies of Solomon's garden. The rich, gleaming, yellow flowers appear in September and October, from one to four to a bulb. They are shaped like a crocus but are larger. This plant grows to a height of from four to six inches, and the dark leaves are strap shaped, from six to eight to a bulb, about one foot long. They appear with the flowers but the shining foliage lasts through the winter. The bulbs should be planted in August, about five or six inches deep, and should not be disturbed until they become crowded. Plant in a rich, well drained soil in full sun, near the front of the flower border. North of Philadelphia they should have some slight winter protection.

SUN ROSE

The sun rose (*Helianthemum Chamaecistus*) also known as yellow cistus, is a procumbent plant, usually with yellow flowers about one inch across. The flowers are commonly in clusters, bloom all summer and are followed by capsular fruit. There are many garden varieties, some with crimson flowers with yellow eyes, others are purplish red and purplish pink; sometimes the foliage is green, and sometimes gray. The plants form dense mats in the rockery and flower border. In the north, they should be heavily mulched in winter. Propagation is by division, by greenwood cuttings and by seeds which germinate readily.

TULIP

A red tulip (*Tulipa montana*), common in the Holy Land, is believed by many authorities to have been the rose of the Bible. This particular species of tulip is seldom listed in American catalogs, but surely any handsome red tulip can stand in its stead in our Bible gardens. The wild stock from which our cultivated tulip comes is lost beyond recovery. Tulips were first cultivated by the Turks, and these cultivated tulips traveled to Europe. Our modern tulips may have the blood of *Tulipa montana* in them, but no one will ever be sure.

Tulip bulbs should be planted in the fall before freezing weather—in September or December in the latitude of the New York region. They will grow in any well drained soil, if the soil is rich with leaf mold and well rotted cow manure. Fresh manure should never be used near bulbs of any sort. Work the soil to a depth of twelve inches, then plant the bulbs from four to six inches deep—to the bottom of the bulbs—and from four to nine inches apart. During winter, the beds should be covered with leaves, dry forest litter, or other light material.

Tulips may remain in the ground for several years if the tops are not cut off, and if the maturing leaves are not smothered by other plants. They often lose their color, and the flowers may diminish in size, but they remain healthy and flourishing.

For pot culture—winter and spring bloom—a good soil mixture is of two parts of fine garden loam, to one of well rotted manure, mixed with clean sand. Fill the pots lightly, press the bulbs into the soil, leaving only the tips exposed. Then press the soil firmly, and water freely. Bury in the soil outdoors, or in ashes or sand, or place in a dark, cool cellar until bulbs root, which will take from five to eight weeks. Bring the pots to the light gradually.

VIOLET

The garden or sweet violet (*Viola odorata*), the parent of the florists' violet, is native to the fields of Palestine and was, surely, among the flowers included in that oft-used phrase, the "flowers of the field."

WATER-LILY

The water-lilies of Egypt grew, too, in the waters of Palestine, and some were, no doubt, cultivated in Solomon's garden. There are several references in the Song of Solomon to "feeding among the lilies." Water-lilies are, of course, favorite food of deer and other animals that wade out into the water to eat them, but the seeds, roots and stalks of water-lilies were common articles of food for the people of the East.

There was "lily work" on the Temple of Solomon: "And the chapiters that were upon the top of the pillars were of lily work in the porch, four cubits . . . and upon the top of the pillars was lily work . . . and the brim thereof was wrought like the brim of a cup, with flowers of lilies" (*I Kings 7:19, 22, 26*). This ornamentation was probably in form of rosettes.

The general consensus of opinion is that the motif was furnished by the water-lily, and that the water-lilies of all possible references are those known to us as white and blue lotus, listed botanically as *Nymphaea alba* and *N. caerulea* and *N. Lotus*. These water-lilies were found in sculptured forms, also in ancient Egyptian tombs.

The white lotus (*N. Lotus*) has leaves which are from twelve to twenty inches across and the white flowers are from five to ten inches across, opening from half past seven in the evening until eleven in the morning.

The blue lotus (*N. caerulea*) has leaves almost as large, and flowers that are from three to six inches across, opening for three days, from half past seven in the morning until noon. Both the white and the blue lotus once floated in profusion on the waters of the Nile, but today they are rare. The white water-lily (*N. alba*) is usually regarded as the European white water-lily. It is robust, with roundish leaves which are red when very young. Several varieties and hybrids are grown in America. Flowers are white—in the type—and open from seven in the morning until four in the afternoon.

Water-lilies need water, rich alluvial soil, and clear sunlight. Often ponds are too shaded for the lilies to thrive. Let the trees remain, but choose open spots for lilies. In the artificial pond, place the lilies in boxes filled with rich soil.

WILLOW HERB

Willow herb (*Epilobium hirsutum*) is often found in old-fashioned gardens. It is a stout, hairy plant, growing from two to four feet high. The showy spikes of flowers bloom from June until August. This plant will make a rank growth planted in moist places; propagation is by division or seeds.

6

Land of Corn

"BEHOLD, a sower went forth to sow . . ."

So begins the first parable spoken by Jesus, providing another proof that our study of Bible plants brings us, again and again, through the common ways of nature, to passages of deep spiritual significance.

The imagery through which Jesus expressed his ideas of the growth of the gospel is as real in America today as it was in Palestine almost two thousand years ago. Today, our great Middle Western wheatfields are plowed and sown by machinery, but the symbolism of the seeds as related to the gospel is still the same. Some seeds fall in good earth and produce "an hundredfold"; others are devoured by wild birds or the neighbors' fowl; some fail to grow in the sub-soil of eroded farms; others are crowded out by weeds.

When our study of Bible plants brings us to the common cereals and legumes—the wheat, barley, millet, lentils, beans and pulse—included by translators in the generic word "corn," we come to some of the most important of Scriptural plants; plants at the basis of civilization today as they were thousands of years ago. Today, while part of our world struggles with a wheat surplus, armies elsewhere contend for the wheatfields; and the fate of nations will now, as always, be decided by the supply of bread.

Wheat and barley, because they were among the first plants to be cultivated by man, tell the story of civilization. The sowing of seed to produce a crop was the first step in changing man's existence from nomadic wandering to settled life. Then culture of the soil led to culture of the mind and heart. Settling of the land introduced social relationships; instead of fighting over animal prey, men had to learn to live with each other and to acquire the rudiments of moral behavior.

The transition from hunting, to herding, to farming was gradual. When the Bible people were roaming desert tribes, in search of green pastures for their herds and flocks, they were already cultivating crops of corn. The dry desert offered few locations in which corn would grow, but between the desert and the sea was that fertile, well-watered strip called Canaan, and though it was coveted by more than one tribe of desert nomads, it was only natural that God should mark this land for His own, and promise it to His faithful servant, Abraham.

Many generations were to pass, however, before the seed of Abraham actually conquered Canaan so that they could settle in it peacefully and devote themselves to the cultivation of its hillsides, valleys and plains. During the lifetime of Abraham, Isaac and Jacob, the Hebrew tribes hardly penetrated beyond the borders of the coveted country, for they were not strong enough to wrest it from the heathen. They pitched their tents on the fringe of it and raised a crop of corn; but in years of famine they migrated to Egypt where grain could be bought.

In spite of the bad years, they must have prospered,

because both Abraham and Isaac were rich men. Their wealth in sheep and oxen was augmented by good crops; Isaac reaped "an hundredfold" (*Gen. 26:12*). Although wheat and barley were their principal agricultural crops, they must also have cultivated the lentils that made pottage, the vine that produced wine, and the olive that produced its fatness, for Isaac's blessing on his son was "God give thee of the dew of heaven, and the fatness of the earth, and plenty of corn and wine" (*Gen. 27:28*). In the days of Jacob, it appears that almond trees were cultivated, for almonds were among the presents sent to Egypt during the famine.

In these early days of Bible history, it is the references to corn that are most revealing. From the days when Joseph dreamed that he and his brethren were binding sheaves of corn in the field, and his sheaf arose to receive the homage of all the rest (*Gen. 37:7*), events of vast consequence occur and the story of Jacob's tribe is joined to the long history of Egypt. For Joseph was able to interpret Pharaoh's dream of the seven fat ears of corn which were devoured by the seven withered ears (*Gen. 41:5-7*), as a forecast of the seven years of plenty which were to be followed by seven years of want. Not only could he chart the cycle of prosperity and hard times, Joseph was able to plan ways to meet the danger, relieve the lack, and save both Pharaoh and the people.

Joseph was made lord over all Egypt. He gathered the corn as the sand of the sea (*Gen. 41:41, 49*) during the seven years of plenty, and stored it in town and country. He prevented a dire famine, and as food administrator he became powerful enough to change the whole economy of Egypt, and alter the course of history for his people.

There is still dispute over how much Joseph learned from Egypt, and how much he taught the Egyptians, as they had been taught much by their own great river. For centuries, the annual overflow of Nile water and mud had produced a rhythm in agriculture and in the work of man that amounted almost to science. The Nile fertilized the fields each year, but men had to dig ditches, and gradually they evolved the elements of engineering with which to irrigate a land where there was no rain. Egyptian slaves toiled with block and tackle, worked treadmill and water wheel, performed miracles of artifice while the Hebrews were seeking pastures for their sheep.

Egyptians planned their agriculture and food supply from year to year. The dreamer, Joseph, was inspired to make a fourteen-year-plan, a bolder move in long-term planning than modern social and economic reformers will attempt. Joseph brought to the engineering problem of Egypt the single-mindedness of the Hebrew worshiper of one God. To Joseph, it was plain that the great river came from God, and that the water it supplied was to be used for the good of all.

Just what Joseph accomplished as an engineer, the Bible does not say in detail; that he did install successful irrigation projects, more than three thousand years before the building of the Assouan dam, is still a tradition in the Nile valley. The fat years were fat because Joseph's system of water control was so far-reaching that bumper crops of corn were grown.

The Bible does tell us, however, what Joseph did

about the grain which was produced. He stored it in the days of plenty, and, when crops failed, sold it for Pharaoh. Purchasers brought money, they bartered flocks and lands, and finally sold themselves into bondage for bread; but they survived the famine (*Gen. 47:13-26*).

Were Joseph's corn laws humane or the reverse?

The answer depends upon whether the people who sold their land to Pharaoh were small farmers or feudal landholders. Historians tell us that in the land of ancient Egypt the great majority of people were slaves and did not own land; so it must have been the feudal lords who sacrificed their property to the central government. The slaves merely changed one master for another; but under Joseph they were elevated to the status of sharecroppers who received four-fifths of the yield which they produced (*Gen. 47:24*), a percentage for which present-day tenants in Egypt or America would be grateful.

It was during this famine period that Joseph's brethren came to him for corn, and there was a reconciliation between them. With the permission of Pharaoh, Joseph was able to move the whole tribe of Jacob to the green pasture land of Goshen in Egypt (*Gen. 47:6*). At last the tribe of Jacob, now the tribe of Israel, had a land which it could occupy without molestation, where it could begin to become a nation. That this move had the blessing of God is apparent; for God appeared to Jacob in a vision and said: "Fear not to go down into Egypt; for I will there make of thee a great nation: I will go down with thee into Egypt; and I will also surely bring thee up again" (*Gen. 46:3, 4*).

Before the move was made, however, it was clear that the sojourn was one day to end; and under a later ruler who knew not Joseph, the struggle in Egypt was to be a bitter one. While Joseph was a power in the land, the Children of Israel were well favored. But after his death and after a change in the line of kings, the Israelites were no longer welcome. They had grown and prospered too much, and Pharaoh was afraid that they would become too powerful. So he made slaves of them and put them to work building pyramids and irrigation canals, made possible by Joseph's nationalization of the land.

It was at this stage of history that the Israelites learned, by sad experience, that the centralized government which worked well under Joseph could become the instrument of tyranny under subsequent rulers. Later Pharaohs, as owners of the land, proved no fairer masters than the feudal overlords. Once again the tribe must move; this time surely to that land, long promised, which was owned neither by a Pharaoh nor by a princely proprietor, but by God.

The Israelites asked for no great wealth, no royal monuments or luxury; their vision was of a land of small homes, where each family might raise wheat and barley for bread, and sit at peace in the cool of the evening, under its own vines and fig trees. As the days of Egyptian slavery passed, this yearning for a homeland grew until the people were ready again to march in search of that Promised Land so long dreamed of but never enjoyed.

After many years of cruel bondage, Moses was chosen by God to deliver his people from Egypt, to lead them through the "waste, howling wilderness" into the land which the Lord had promised their fathers. In this land, marked by God as His own, the wandering Children of Israel were to settle, to become a peaceful agricultural nation. Not only was the Promised Land now described as one of "wheat and barley" wherein the people could "eat bread without scarceness" (*Deut. 8:8, 9*); it was henceforth to be described as a land of "corn, wine and oil." This phrase, used by Moses in describing the blessings of the Promised Land (*Deut. 7:13*), appears over and over in the Bible, a constant proof of the bounty of God.

Although Abraham, Isaac and Jacob had known that the Promised Land was one which depended directly upon God for its abundant harvests, the Children of Israel who now went in to possess it had to learn this truth. For they were the descendants of men and women who knew no country but Egypt, and Egypt was very different from Palestine. In Egypt there was no rain from heaven. Water was furnished to the fields by man; lifted from the Nile by wheels and buckets, the wheel worked by a treadmill on which slaves labored long hours in the sun under the lash of the overseer. The system of ditching was simple, so that water running through the shallow channels in the fields could often be diverted from one channel to another by breaking down or closing up the separating ridges with the foot.

But Palestine was no place to be watered by a movement of the foot; it was no flat, rainless, treeless land, such as Egypt. Palestine was a land which God watched over for twelve months in the year. "The land, whither ye go to possess it," said Moses to his people, "is a land of hills and valleys, and drinketh water of the rain of heaven: a land which the Lord thy God careth for" (*Deut. 11:11-12*).

It was a land in which God would send the rain in its due season, "the first rain and the latter rain, that thou mayest gather in thy corn, and thy wine, and thine oil" (*Deut. 11:14*).

The rain of heaven, sent by God, came during the six winter months and although it came frequently during this period it was, nevertheless, referred to as the former and the latter rain. The former rain began about the end of October and watered the whole land, preparing it for the sowing of seed. It became gradually heavier until the end of December, and then continued during intervals until spring. The showers in March and April were called the latter rain; they came at the time when crops were ripening, providing the moisture necessary to make them mature.

Not only did God send the rain, He sent it at the right time and according to a definite law. So confident were the people of the early and latter rain on the expected dates, that rain during harvest was regarded as a phenomenon as well as a disaster. In Proverbs (*26:1*), snow in summer and rain in harvest are similes for unseemly happenings. In the first book of Samuel, the prophet called upon the Lord to send thunder and rain in time of wheat harvest, as a rebuke to the people who desired a king (*I Sam. 12:16-18*).

Naturally this need for water, supplied by God, led to a symbolic interpretation of water as truth, God's word, clear and cleansing and elemental. "My doctrine shall drop as the rain . . . as the small rain upon the tender herb, and as the showers upon the grass" (*Deut. 32:2*). "And he shall come unto us as the rain, as the latter and former rain unto the earth" (*Hos. 6:3*).

Harvest was a time for thanksgiving, and the Lord, Himself, gave Moses instructions for the celebrations which were to be observed during the agricultural year. The Feast of Unleavened Bread, the Feasts of Weeks, or Pentecost, and the Feast of Tabernacles, were to be times of joy and praise to God who blessec His people with the fruit of the earth.

At the beginning of the harvest came the Feast of Unleavened Bread, during which the priest waved a sheaf of new corn before the altar. Fifty days later, Pentecost began with the offering of two loaves made of new wheat. Last in the season came the Feast of Tabernacles, celebrating both the grain harvest and the vintage.

The joy in the harvest season was to be shared by the poor, for God's bounty was for all His people. This attitude prompted such customs as leaving to the poor and to the stranger the gleaning of the fields, vineyards and oliveyards (*Lev. 23:22*). Had it not been for this, Ruth must have stood hungry amidst the alien corn. A similar extension of consideration to animals forbade the muzzling of oxen treading the grain; the Lord would provide, of His bounty, enough for all His creatures, man and beast.

Every seventh year was to be a Sabbath unto the land, just as every seventh day was a day of rest for man and beast. Not only was the land permitted to rest, to remain uncultivated during its Sabbath, but its natural produce was to be left so "that the poor of thy people may eat: and what they leave the beasts of the field shall eat." The Sabbath rest was decreed for grain field, vineyard and olive grove.

Laws of land tenure were carefully designed to keep the people mindful that God was the source of their blessings. The land belonged to God, and His people were guests and sojourners upon His land. "The land shall not be sold forever," were the words of the Lord, "for the land is mine" (*Lev. 25:23*). Therefore, all land reverted to its original owners every fiftieth year, called the Year of Jubilee, and when land was bought or sold it was with the Year of Jubilee in mind, for the price varied with the number of years to Jubilee. In this fiftieth year, "ye shall return every man unto his possession . . . ye shall not therefore oppress one another; but thou shalt fear thy God" (*Lev. 25:10, 17*).

Although slavery, the very worst kind of oppression, existed among the Bible people as among all the ancients, the slave was freed in Jubilee Year, and in Sabbatical years between. The slave was not only to be given his liberty, if he so desired, but he was to be helped to make a start on his own. "Thou shalt furnish him liberally out of thy flock, and out of thy floor, and out of thy winepress: of that wherewith the Lord hath blessed thee should thou give unto him" (*Deut. 15:14*).

Although the methods of agriculture and the laws about land and slavery of Bible times seem to belong to a day very different from ours, the basic social and economic problems seem the same. Today we are still trying to solve the problems of land ownership, of a fair deal for its tenants; we are still coping with supply and demand and distribution of wealth. Social progress, there has been, in the intervening centuries; but this progress had been largely due to the foundation stones of justice and freedom laid down in those early Bible times. And, as has been pointed out by many Bible students, in the doctrine of the brotherhood of man, preached by Jesus Christ, were the seeds of the movement that eventually was to set all men free.

BARLEY

Barley and wheat were the two staple cereal crops of both Palestine and Egypt, and were the most important of all crops referred to as corn. Barley, the less expensive, was widely used by the poor for bread. Mentioned many times in the Bible, barley makes its first appearance as an Egyptian crop which was "in the ear" when the plague of hail smote the land of the Nile destroying this valuable food (*Exo. 9:31*).

Barley, as one of the plants of our Bible garden, will lead us directly to the Book of Ruth which gives us an intimate and appealing picture of life on the land at its best. The scene of the barley harvest in chapter two not only gives us details of the work of the day, but reveals the friendly, brotherly spirit which existed between Boaz, the lord who owned the land, and his workers and the gleaners who came to his field for charity.

Reapers cut the standing barley with sickles, maidens bind the grain into sheaves, and gleaners follow behind, picking up the leavings. An overseer is on hand to manage the work of the day but, nevertheless, the owner comes to visit the field and to exchange greetings with his servants and, upon occasion, to join with them in the noonday meal.

"The Lord be with you," is the greeting spoken by Boaz to his men.

"The Lord bless you," is their answer.

One day there is a new gleaner in the field, a woman. Boaz inquires of his overseer: "Whose damsel is this?" And when he learns that she is a widow and a stranger, he extends to her a special invitation to glean in his field. He tells the young men who are working in the field to be careful of their language and to treat this woman with respect. He instructs the maidens binding sheaves to leave extra ears of barley for this deserving stranger. And, at mealtime, Ruth is invited to join Boaz and the workers in the noonday meal, which consists of bread dipped in vinegar and parched corn.

The Book of Ruth is richly rewarding in its revelation of character and domestic love; and as a story of the mood and spirit of the agricultural life of Bible times, it has no peer in Scripture.

Barley is mentioned many times as a growing plant, as barley meal, barley bread, barley cakes and barley loaves. The most famous bread loaves of the Bible were made of barley. Jesus had come from the sea of Galilee up into the mountains and was followed by great crowds of people. It was the time of the passover, and Jesus said to his disciples:

"Whence shall we buy bread, that these may eat?"

A lad in the crowd had five barley loaves and two small fishes, but, as Andrew pointed out, what are they among so many? But Jesus took the loaves, and blessed them, and the bread and the fishes fed the multitude of five thousand. And after everyone had had his fill, the disciples were able to fill twelve baskets with the fragments that remained (*John 6:1-14*).

Barley (*Hordeum distichon*) can be grown easily from seed. It makes an attractive patch of vivid green, grown in clumps in the garden. No grain which has been cultivated by man equals barley in the extent of climatic variation under which it will grow. It will bear heat and drought better than any grain and attains its maturity so rapidly that even the short summers of northern latitudes provide sufficient sun.

BEAN

The broad bean (*Vicia faba* or *Faba vulgaris*) is the bean of the Bible although today it has many names, and sometimes is called Windsor bean, Scotch bean and horse bean. Today, the broad bean is grown mostly as a forage crop, although it furnishes food for man as well as beast. It was the only edible bean known in Europe before the time of Christopher Columbus.

This bean may have been originally a native of Persia. It was extensively cultivated as a food in western Asia in very early times, but its actual land of origin is obscure. We know that it was early cultivated in Egypt, since beans of this sort have been found in mummy coffins. Even today the shores of the Nile are often fragrant with the sweet perfume of the bean fields. In Syria this bean is widely cultivated as fodder for cattle.

Beans are mentioned twice in the Bible: "wheat, and barley, and flour, and parched corn, and beans, and lentiles, and parched pulse" (*II Sam. 17:28*) were brought to King David's hungry army; and Ezekiel mentions beans, along with seeds and grains, as the ingredients of the bread which would be made during the siege of Jerusalem (*Eze. 4:9*).

The broad bean will grow easily in gardens in the northern part of the United States where summers are not too long and hot. It is grown commercially in Canada. This strong, erect anuual, from two to four feet in height, has flowers that are white or penciled with lilac streaks and marked with a black spot. The pods are flat and enclose large seeds. When grown in the Bible garden, place the plant in an inconspicuous position, where its dense green foliage will fill a spot with green, but where its coarse leaves will not hide more delicate plants.

LENTIL

These peas were mentioned in the Samuel and Ezekiel references given in the preceding paragraphs on beans. And we read that one of David's mighty men stood in the midst of a field of lentils and defended it and slew the Philistines who had gathered there (*II Sam. 23:11*).

The most discussed mention of lentils is in connection with the red pottage made by Jacob. In Genesis (*25: 20-34*), we read the story of Isaac and Rebekah and their twin sons, Esau and Jacob. It is told that Esau, the first born, was a hunter and man of the field. Jacob was a thinker, and clever enough to devise a scheme for tempting Esau to sell his right as the eldest son. Jacob brewed a broth of lentils, so that the odor of it would strike Esau as he came home from the fields, faint and hungry. Esau, valuing the desire of the moment above future benefits, traded his birthright for the mess of pottage.

The lentil (*Lens esculenta*) is one of the most important food plants of the human race. It is an annual, much branched, with numerous oval leaves, and small flowers, white or pale blue. The pods are short, broad and very flat, containing two flat seeds. The seeds should be sown in drills in March, and keep best if left in the pods when harvested.

MILLET

Millet is not a cereal but it has long been cultivated by man for its seeds, which are the smallest of all grass seeds; each head produces such a tremendous number that the plant received the specific name of *miliaceum*. There are large fields of millet in Palestine and Egypt even today. Millet is one of the ingredients of the bread which Ezekiel made as a sign of the coming siege of Jerusalem. "Take thou also unto thee wheat, and barley, and beans, and lentiles, and millet, and fitches, and put them in one vessel" (*Eze. 4:9*). The word fitches of this reference is considered a mis-translation, the true meaning being "spelt," which is an inferior variety of wheat.

Millet (*Panicum miliaceum*) is a stout grass, with broad leaves; it bears dense clusters of small seeds. It can be grown in clumps in the Bible garden where flowers and vegetables are planted together in a mixed border.

WHEAT

Although wheat was the most important food plant in Bible days as it is today, it was then not so available to all people. As we have already noted, barley was much used in bread and cakes, but today, as a source of flour it has been almost completely supplanted by wheat.

Wheat in the Bible garden can lead us to a study of the agricultural economy that so greatly influenced the early Hebrews, as well as to the meaning of the parables of Jesus. In the parable of the sower and of the wheat and the tares, Jesus made use of the plant that was so important an ingredient of bread. And when we grow wheat, as well as other Bible corn, we can certainly let our interest in them lead us to the many references to bread which is so important in the spiritual symbolism of the Scriptures. Jesus missed no opportunity to bring home his teachings with references to this essential supply of food. That the gospel itself was the true bread from heaven he made plain; it was to be divided among his followers, broken symbolically with the disciples, and in every way regarded as a daily necessity of life.

Wheat (*Triticum aestivum*) can be sown in the garden so that it will grow in clumps, or as a hedge or screen. It should be staked or surrounded by a light wire when tall. The dried wheat, on stalks, can be effectively used as decoration in a church celebration, and in arrangements of Bible plants. The tare (*Lolium temulentum*), called darnel grass, is the only grass known with poisonous properties. The tare resembles wheat so closely that it is impossible to distinguish between them until the wheat is in fruit. Seeds of darnel grass cannot be easily obtained, since they are of no commercial or ornamental value, although the grass will grow readily enough in this country.

Pistachios flourish in the United States even as they did in Palestine thousands of years ago.

7

Perfumes and Precious Woods

FRANKINCENSE and myrrh are associated in our minds with the birth of Jesus. Although Jesus was born in a humble manger in Bethlehem, the wise men recognized him as King, and brought him gifts befitting a royal person—frankincense and myrrh, which ranked in value with the third gift, gold.

Later in life, during His ministry, the feet of Jesus were anointed with spikenard "very costly" and, when the fragrant ointment was poured forth, the room was filled with the odor of it. Later still, after the crucifixion, Nicodemus laid away the body of Jesus, winding it in soft linens and putting a mixture of myrrh and aloes and sweet spices in the folds.

The words frankincense, myrrh, aloes and spikenard stir the mind to thoughts of Jesus, but few of us realize the important rôle the perfume-producing plants play all through the Scriptures, and the interesting aspects of history to which they lead us. The fact that frankincense and myrrh, balm, aloes, spikenard, calamus, cinnamon and cassia were in use in the Holy Land and Egypt is proof that trade and commerce with distant lands existed even in earliest times. For, as we know now, the fragrant gums, resins, oils, powders, bark and balsams, called by these names, were produced by various trees and shrubs and grasses which grew as far away as

India and China. These perfume-producing plants did not grow in Palestine, except as exotics in Solomon's garden. The three precious woods included in this chapter—algum, ebony and thyine wood—are further proof of trade with distant countries.

Also, under the general heading of perfume, we must consider both the incense and the ointments of Bible times. Perfumes were used in religious and secular life, and the ingredients of holy incense and holy ointment were made not only of the most costly fragrant substances, but according to the secret formulas of professional perfumers, known as apothecaries in those days.

In the wilderness, Moses received instructions to use myrrh and frankincense, cinnamon, calamus, cassia, galbanum and sweet spices in the making of holy compounds (*Ex. 30:23,24,34*). That these compounds were to be especially composed for the Lord is firmly stressed:

"And thou shalt make it a perfume, a confection after the art of the apothecary, tempered together, pure and holy: and thou shalt beat some of it very small, and put of it before the testimony in the tabernacle of the congregation, where I will meet with thee: it shall be unto you most holy. And as for the perfume which thou shalt make, ye shall not make to yourselves according to the composition thereof: it shall be unto thee holy for the Lord. Whosoever shall make like unto that, to smell thereto, shall even be cut off from his people" (*Ex. 30:35-37*).

One of the special secrets was the identity of the herb which was used in making holy incense. This herb made the smoke rise in a tall column, directly toward heaven, before dispersing.

The smoke of incense, ascending toward God, was symbolic of the prayers of men as they rose to heaven, so that the burning incense was a symbol of intercession with God. Aaron, during the plague in the wilderness, interceded with God on behalf of the people by burning incense as an atonement for their sin. He passed through the congregation, the incense burning in his censer, "and he stood between the dead and the living, and the plague was stayed" (*Numb. 16:46-48*). David, praying to the Lord, says: "Let my prayer be set forth before thee as incense" (*Ps. 141:2*). The symbolism is carried further in the vision of the holy city where there are "golden vials full of odors, which are the prayers of saints" (*Rev. 5:8*).

The burning of incense, both morning and evening, was part of the daily service in the Temple of Jerusalem. While the sacrifice of the lamb occurred outside the Temple proper, before the porch, the incense was offered inside, on the golden altar which stood before the veil of the Holy of Holies. Only the officiating priest could enter this sanctuary, and he must enter alone. The congregation prayed outside the walls of the Temple while the incense burned within: "And the whole multitude of people were praying without at the time of incense" (*Luke 1:10*).

To moderns of the Occident, perfume as incense, or as a liquid luxury to sprinkle on the person, seems to be a mildly intoxicating pleasure with little or no practical value. But to the ancients of the Orient, perfume was a necessity, associated with cleanliness and purity. In a world where there were no modern devices of sanitation for preventing and checking infection and other agencies

injurious to health, incense and ointments were absolutely essential. To perfume once meant "to fumigate."
Although this meaning is now obsolete, it does suggest
its former use. The burning of incense in homes and
public places was a valuable disinfectant, and the clean,
spicy fumes of forest gums must have made more bear-
able the odors of a city like Jerusalem where evil smells
were bound to exist if references to horse gate, sheep
gate, fish gate and dung gate are at all descriptive.
(*Neh. 3:1, 3, 13, 28*).

With only an elemental knowledge of chemistry employed in the making of compounds, and no refrigera-
tion or vacuum packing to preserve freshness, the use of
spices and various fragrant substances as preservatives
for food and toilet requisites was a necessity. It was found
that the addition of certain gums, or distillation of
leaves and bark, not only made the oil in a vessel more
pleasant to smell and taste, it also kept the oil from
turning rancid.

Thus as antiseptics, preservatives, medicines and personal luxuries, incense and ointments made life more
livable in a day when the principles of hygiene were not
understood or so easily enacted as they are today. Unguents made of olive oil and flavored with aromatic
substances, or made of costlier oils as a base, were in
constant use as an indispensable part of the daily toilet.
To leave off the anointing of the person was a sign of
mourning; it was resumed as soon as mourning was
over. Unguents were not used as substitutes for bodily
cleanliness, as they were later in medieval Europe, but
were applied after the bath, not only for protection of

the skin, but to make the person smell sweet: "Ointment and perfume rejoice the heart" (*Prov. 27:9*).

Ointments were rubbed upon the face and head, body and feet. Perfumes were kept in sealed jars or cruses; thousands of these, unearthed in Palestine and Syria, suggest a trade relatively as important as today's cosmetic business. The more valuable unguents were in containers made of alabaster, like the one which contained the ointment of spikenard which was broken to anoint Jesus (*Mark 14:3*).

Women wore small flasks of myrrh which, suspended from a chain, rested upon the breast; the maiden in the Song of Solomon (*1:13*) uses this imagery in speaking of her well beloved who is to her as a "bundle of myrrh." And in an earlier verse (*1:3*), the name of the beloved has the savor of "an ointment poured forth," because it was when the alabaster boxes and flasks poured forth their contents that their fragrance was released.

From Egypt, the people of Palestine brought the use of perfume in the last rites for the dead. In the Old Testament in the account of the death of King Asa, they "laid him in the bed which was filled with sweet odors and divers kinds of spices prepared by the apothecaries' art: and they made a very great burning for him" (*II Chron. 16:14*). In the New Testament, women prepared spices and ointments which they carried to the tomb of Jesus (*Luke 23:56*), and Nicodemus brought a mixture of myrrh and aloes. Here again the use of incense, perfume and ointments is obviously practical.

The plants that furnished the gums, oils and resins that were used in making perfume products grew, for the most part, in India, China, Africa and Arabia. They reached the people of the Mediterranean shores by long, slow passage in merchant ships and by camel caravans. It was to a caravan of Ishmaelites, "bearing spicery and balm and myrrh" to Egypt, that Joseph was sold by his brothers (*Gen. 37:25*). Although these expensive products were always available to the Hebrews, in the early days, they were used only as necessities of religious and daily life. During the birth of the nation, the shepherd-farmer-warrior was far too busy to indulge in lavish living. He was fleet as a lion, swift as an eagle, and did not dally for long periods on a perfumed couch as later became the custom. His earliest desire was for peace, not perfumed luxury. His mind and heart looked forward to the time when each man could sit under his vine and fig tree and not make war.

When the day of prolonged peace arrived, however, his energy was released for building up the prosperity of the country. Agriculture was the first to flourish, but trade also began to be resumed in the land. Before the Israelites conquered Canaan, trade had been fairly active in the hands of the heathen, especially since the plains of this little land furnished the highways for the exchange of goods from the Eastern world. David, having consolidated the empire, established relations with Hiram of Tyre, and laid the foundations for the building of the Temple and for the expansion of trade and commerce that was to develop greatly during the reign of Solomon, his son.

Solomon was ambitious to carry through the plans of his father, and also to make his own name shine in the East. As king, he modeled himself after Oriental potentates of other countries, but his desire was to be the most splendid of them all. He gained control of several caravan routes, and established a port on the Red Sea so that he could traffic with Ophir and India. Money flowed into the little kingdom and people began to get rich. Not only was foreign commerce profitable, but trade within the country offered attractive opportunities for making a living so that bright, young country boys went to town to make their fortune.

But trade with other nations brought knowledge of foreign customs. It brought contact with people who were worldly and luxury loving. The incense and ointments that had once been a consecrated part of life, now also became a self-indulgence of the rich. Country life and city life began to grow farther and farther apart. This contrast is celebrated in the exquisite love poetry of the Song of Songs or Song of Solomon. The simplicity of the shepherd stands out in contrast to the grandeur of the king, and the uncultivated beauty of the Lebanon countryside is pictured in contrast to the artificial splendor of the exotic garden. The charm of the bride is described in terms of the garden and its fountains, and in terms of the plants which exhaled such exquisite fragrance: "Camphire with spikenard. Spikenard and saffron; calamus and cinnamon, with all the trees of frankincense; myrrh and aloes with all the chief spices" (*Sol. 4:13, 14*). These plants may or may not have been grown by Solomon, but the figurative use made of them here reveals to us that their perfumes were part of the extravagance of kings.

The use of incense is revealed in the account of the royal procession. The betrothed is borne through the

streets on his litter, with pillars of smoke rising round
it and "all the powders of the merchant"—all the perfumes known to the period—perfumed the air. Whether
we accept this group of poems as one in which Solomon
actually plays a part, or as a group of songs sung during
the wedding week in which any pair of betrothed lovers
play a royal part, its imagery tells us a great deal about
royal gardens and royal pomp and ceremony.

Solomon, by expanding the horizons of his little
country, made it susceptible to heathen influences, and
he himself married many heathen wives, indulgently
permitting them to bring their gods with them. In time,
he became confused in his religious beliefs, and in his
old age, began to lose his grip on the people. National
unity began to disintegrate and after his death, troubled
years followed thick and fast.

Solomon, in his younger days of wisdom, had perhaps
envisioned a great future for his nation. But, in execut-
ing his plans, he forgot the rights of private citizens,
he overburdened them with taxes, and had to resort
to conscripted labor to build the Temple.

His son, who succeeded him on the throne, had none
of the earlier wisdom of his father. When the people
came to ask that the heavy yoke imposed by Solomon
be lifted, Rehoboam foolishly replied:

"I will add to your yoke: my father hath chastised
you with whips, but I will chastise you with scorpions"
(*I Kings 12:11*).

The fortunes of the little nation vacillated between
good and bad under a series of unfortunate rulers, and,
each time there was a period of peace, material prosperity seemed to increase at the cost of spiritual upright-

ness. Upper classes seemed to prosper at the expense of lower, city people at the expense of country people. The Year of Jubilee, which had been the ideal for writing off injustices in an agricultural country, now failed to work or was forgotten in a rapidly changing world where power was concentrated in the city. Isaiah complained about the forming of large estates: "Woe unto them that join house to house, that lay field to field" (*Isa. 5:8*). And Micah complained that the rich coveted fields and took them by violence (*Mi. 2:2*). Amos, decrying the sins of the times, complained that the people were lying around on beds of ivory, stretching themselves upon their couches, playing music, drinking wine and anointing themselves with all the chief ointments (*Amos 6:4-6*).

When calamity befell the nation, when internal and political bickering and foreign invasion kept the country in turmoil, many of the people lost their single-mindedness about God. Perhaps their God was unable to protect and save them from their enemies after all; perhaps the gods of their heathen neighbors had better be propitiated. Through fear and lack of faith, the incense, which had once been offered only to the true God, was now burned on altars to false deities. This was the practice of which the prophets spoke so sternly: "A people that provoketh me to anger continually to my face; that sacrificeth in gardens, and burneth incense upon altars of brick" (*Isa. 65:3*). And Jeremiah said: "Then shall the cities of Judah and the inhabitants of Jerusalem go, and cry unto the gods unto whom they offer incense: but they shall not save them at all in the time of their trouble" (*Jer. 11:12*).

Unfortunately, many of the plants of this chapter are not available for American gardens, although cinnamon and cassia and a few others can be raised in the South or as greenhouse plants. A few of these plants have been brought to the West Indies where they are now raised commercially, but the world today is still dependent upon the countries of the East and Far East for its supply of these fragrant substances. Today, animal odors are widely used in making perfume and incense, a practice unknown to the ancients, but the plant substances are still greatly in demand.

Aloes

Aloes were used in various kinds of perfume, incense and scented powders, and the word itself appears in both the Old and the New Testament. In Psalms, all the garments of the King are described as smelling of "myrrh, aloes and cassia" (*Ps. 45:8*). A bed is perfumed with "myrrh, aloes and cinnamon" (*Prov. 7:17*). And aloes are named as one of the plants of the garden of Solomon (*Sol. 4:14*).

These aloes are believed to refer to the eaglewood tree (*Aquilaria agallocha*), a lofty tree, a hundred or more feet tall, native of India and Malaya. It is still often called "aloes wood." The wood is fragrant, especially the darker part, and when in a state of decay is highly valued in perfumery.

Some authorities believe that the Old Testament aloes were white sandalwood (*Santalum album*). This is a native of India and today is generally used by all Oriental nations for its fragrant wood. It is a low tree, resembling a privet. Neither the eaglewood nor sandal-wood is grown in this country.

Balaam compared the tents of the Israelites to "trees of lign aloes which the Lord hath planted" (*Numb. 24:6*), but since the trees mentioned above did not grow in the Holy Land, Balaam could hardly have been referring to them. The Hebrew word used in this verse is one which applies to a number of different trees, how-ever, and must be translated according to the context of the passage in which it appears. Most authorities agree that Balaam was referring to the myrtle and other aromatic trees which were native to Palestine.

The aloes of the New Testament (*John 19:39*), brought by Nicodemus to be used in the burial of the crucified Savior, are from the plant known as *Aloe succotrina*. It is still esteemed in the East for its per-fume, although the drug made from the pulp of the fleshy leaves is used principally in horse medicine in the rest of the world.

This aloe has tubular, red flowers, tipped with green, borne on a dense spike, blooming every year. It is obtainable from nurserymen, and thrives out-of-doors in the warm and arid sections of the country, and is suitable for an outdoor desert garden.

Indoors, the aloe may be grown in pots and plunged out of doors during summer. In winter, it may be grown in a window garden or kept in a cool, light cellar. The soil should be made very porous by addition of a lib-eral proportion of broken bricks or coarse cinders. Do not keep too wet. Re-pot every third or fourth year in the spring. The soil should be made firm about the roots. It is easily propagated from cuttings.

Almug or Algum

The precious wood, called both almug and algum, was imported by King Solomon and used in making the pillars for the house of the Lord, and for making harps and psalteries (*I Kings 10:11, 12*). This timber was brought by sea from Ophir, a mart of exchange for Indian goods. That the wood came from India is practically assured because it was known only by its Indian name of almug or algum, and the tree itself is believed to be red sandalwood (*Pterocarpus santalina*), which is a native of India. Merchandise coming from Ophir, which may have been on the coast of Africa, India, or Arabia, came by ship up the Red Sea.

The red sandalwood is a large leguminous tree with hard and heavy, red wood which takes a fine polish. It is not cultivated in this country, although boxes and other objects made of red sandalwood are obtainable and might represent the tree in a Bible plant display.

Plantations of algum trees may possibly have grown in Lebanon, near Tyre, planted there by Hiram to use for commercial purposes. Solomon asked for algum trees out of Lebanon, but most authorities agree that the word here translated as algum is a mistake, and should have been translated cypress instead (*II Chron. 2:8*).

Balm

"Is there no balm in Gilead?" Jeremiah's (*8:22*) well-known question has made the "balm of Gilead" one of the famous plants of the Bible, yet most authorities are of the opinion that the plant which produced most

of the balm was a native of Arabia, not Gilead, and
known by the impressive name of *Balsamodendrum
gileadense* or *Commiphora opobalsamum*. The balm or
balsam is obtained by making incisions in the stem and
branches of the trees. The exuding sap soon hardens
into small irregular nodules, is collected, and in modern
times shipped to Bombay where it enters the commercial trade.

Other references to balm may be to this same plant
product or to the product of another plant known as
Balanites aegyptiaca which abounds in Egypt, northern
Africa, in the plains of Jericho, and bordering the Dead
Sea. It is a desert-loving plant and is held in veneration
by the Mohammedans in India, where it is also found.
Oil is obtained from this plant by pounding the fruits
and then boiling them.

Another source of the balm of the Bible is the mastick
tree (*Pistacia lentiscus*) which *is* found in Gilead, especially abundant in the rocky country. This tree also
grows in Palestine. Its balm is an exudation of the sap
secured by making incisions in the stem and branches.
Known in commerce as mastick, it is used extensively
in varnish.

This tree is hardy in the warmer sections of the
country, but elsewhere must be grown in pots and set
out only in summer. It is an evergreen, growing to a
height of fifteen feet.

CALAMUS

Calamus grew in the garden of Solomon (*4:14*); it
was among the substances ordered by the Lord for the

holy ointment of the Tabernacle (*Ex. 30:23*); and it was mentioned as one of the products in the markets of Tyre (*Eze. 27:19*).

Opinions differ, but the sweet flag (*Acorus calamus*) and a beardgrass (*Andropogon aromaticus*) have both been suggested as the plants from which calamus came.

Sweet flag looks like iris and is well known to all gardeners; it is a plant of wet places and stream sides, highly aromatic throughout. If planted in an ordinary border, it should be watered freely throughout the summer. It is propagated by division and is easily naturalized.

Beardgrass, or Andropogon grass, is highly odoriferous when bruised; the beardgrass which may have furnished the calamus of the Bible grew in India, but it is kin to our own blue stem, a well known native beardgrass.

CAMPHIRE

The camphire of Solomon's garden is known to us as henna, and is a handsome shrub with clusters of white, rose or yellow flowers, very fragrant. It has pale-green, privetlike leaves and grows from four to ten feet high. It grows in Egypt, Syria, Arabia and northern India, and is now naturalized in the West Indies.

Henna (*Lawsonia inermis*) is hardy out of doors in Florida, and in Southern California. In other sections it should be grown in a pot, wintered in the greenhouse, and set out of doors after danger of frost is past. Young plants may be obtained from nurserymen.

CINNAMON AND CASSIA

These spices, which are two different grades of cinnamon, were used by Moses in the wilderness; they grew in the garden of Solomon, and are named among the wares of Babylon the Great. They are native to India, and cassia bark produces a cinnamon that is inferior to the true cinnamon.

The true cinnamon (*Cinnamomum zeylanicum*) is a low-growing tree with smooth, ash-colored bark and wide spreading branches. The leaves are eight or nine inches long and about two inches wide, bright green above and white beneath. Young shoots are crimson with bark often speckled with deep green and orange spots. The cinnamon of commerce is the inner bark, peeled off trees that are four or five years old. The finest cinnamon comes from the young branches. Oil of cinnamon is made by soaking small broken pieces of bark in sea water for some hours, and then distilling. It was one of the principal ingredients used in the manufacture of precious ointments in the Tabernacle, it was costly and highly prized.

This plant can be grown as a greenhouse plant and as a house plant in a room having a night temperature of 60°. It can be plunged out of doors when warm weather comes. Plant the pot and all in ground in the shade, and keep well watered. It is propagated by cuttings.

The cassia bark tree (*Cinnamomum cassia*) grows to a height of forty feet and has glossy, stiff, long leaves. It grows out of doors in Florida; in other regions it will grow in pots of ordinary soil, well drained and plunged out of doors during summer. The spice is secured by making longitudinal incisions in the bark of the branches. The bark then dries and peels off, rolling itself up into tubes.

EBONY

Ezekiel (*27:15*) mentions ebony as part of the merchandise of Tyre. This tree grew in India and Ceylon and was conveyed by ship up the Red Sea. The outer wood of the ebony is white and soft, but when old, the interior wood becomes hard and black, and constitutes the ebony of commerce, highly valuable for cabinet work, turnery and fancy articles.

The trees are large but slow growing, and have small bell-shaped flowers. Ebony (*Diospyros ebenaster* and *D. ebenum*) can be grown indoors and plunged out of doors in summer. An American relative of the ebony is the common persimmon (*Diospyros virginiana*).

FRANKINCENSE

Frankincense was used by the Children of Israel in the desert (*Ex. 30:34*), and it continues to be mentioned all through the Old Testament. In the New Testament, it is one of the gifts brought by the wise men to the infant Jesus.

Frankincense (*Boswellia thurifera*) is a tree of large size, and this and related species grow in Southern Arabia and on the opposite coast of Africa and in Western India. Pale red or yellow gum exudes from this tree in the form of roundish or oblong drops or "tears," and gives off a strong, balsamic odor when warmed or burned.

GALBANUM

Galbanum was an ingredient of the holy compound used in the Tabernacle (*Ex. 30:34*). The word appears but once, and there is little evidence to support a theory about which plant produced the galbanum of the Scriptures. However, it may have been *Ferula galbaniflura* and related species; this plant is a member of the Carrot family and is native to Persia and Syria.

The plants producing galbanum gum are strong-rooted perennials, their flowering stems reaching several feet in height with alternate, partially sheathing, finely divided leaves, terminated by umbels of yellow or greenish-white flowers. The whole plant abounds with a milky juice which oozes from the joints of old plants and it exudes and hardens from the base of the stem after it has been cut down, and is finally obtained from incisions in the root. Galbanum is at present used in medicine.

MYRRH

Myrrh has been widely known and used in all ages as an ingredient of perfume, medicine, and as a preservative in embalming. The Bible myrrh may have been obtained from a balsam known as *Commiphora myrrha* and *C. erythraea,* and also from the plant known to us as rockrose (*Cistus ladaniferus*).

The balsam (*Commiphora myrrha*) is a large shrub,

or small tree, of Abyssinia, Somaliland, and Arabia. The gum resin oozes naturally from the stems, or as a result of wounding. The pale-yellow liquid gradually solidifies and becomes brown or even black in color. Myrrh from this plant is known as Herabol myrrh. It is used today in tonics, stimulants, antiseptics and is often a constituent of mouthwashes and dentifrices. Sweet myrrh, or Bisabol myrrh, comes from the plant *Commiphora erythraea,* an Arabian species of similar appearance to the *C. myrrha.* Both species are scrubby, stiff-branched and thorny, with oval, plumlike fruit. They grow in rocky places and on limestone hills.

In some of the passages where myrrh is mentioned, it has been translated from a word which means "fragrant gum." Fragrant gum rather than myrrh fits the passage about the Ishmaelites (*Gen. 37:25*), and the passage about gifts sent to Egypt (*Gen. 43:11*). This fragrant gum is believed by many authorities to have come from several species of rockrose or *Cistus*—(*Cistus ladaniferus, C. creticus, C. salvifolius* and *C. villosus*). These plants yield the laudanum of commerce, a viscid gummy exudation, from stems and leaves. It is collected during the heat of the day by drawing over the bushes a bunch of leather thongs, or some woven material, to which the gum adheres. This gum also adheres to the beards of goats as they browse among the bushes, and is later combed out and used.

The rockrose is commonly cultivated in this country. In the North it should be grown in sheltered positions, but even then does not always prove hardy. It is a handsome evergreen, from three to five feet high, with a lovely flower which resembles a big, single rose.

ONYCHA

This substance which is mentioned with galbanum in Exodus (*30:34*), does not offer the commentators much to go on. Many people consider it to be of animal source, those who believe it to be a plant substance identify it with benzoin, a product of the plant *Styrax benzoin* and related species.

Benzoin is exceedingly aromatic, with a vanillalike odor. It is used in medicine as a stimulant, and in the preparation of heavy, sweet perfumes, soap, toilet waters, lotions, tooth powders, incense and fumigating materials. The powder *Styrax benzoin* is used also as a fixative in the making of potpourris.

SAFFRON

Saffron is the product of several species of crocus, especially the blue-flowered *Crocus sativus*. The dried stigmas and tops of the styles are used as a spice and as a dyestuff. These are clipped as soon as the flowers open, and are dried naturally or with artificial heat. It takes four thousand flowers to furnish an ounce of dye. The coloring material is readily soluble in water, so is not used for fabrics. It is, however, much used for coloring medicines and food. Today, saffron is still used as a flavoring material to some extent. Saffron cakes are popular in some parts of England. It is an ingredient of many European dishes, particularly the famous French *bouillabaisse,* and in the Latin-American dish, *arroz con pollo.*

The thistlelike safflower (*Carthamus tinctorius*) is

often used as an adulterant of saffron, and since this
plant is native to India, but also grows in regions of
Palestine and Egypt, it may very well have been so used
in Bible times. This flower is common in the United
States.

SPIKENARD

Spikenard was one of the most precious and costly
substances used by the ancients. It was an ointment of
spikenard that Mary of Bethany used in anointing the
feet of Jesus (*John 12:3-9*), and so costly was it that
Judas Iscariot said: "Why was not this ointment sold
for three hundred pence and given to the poor?"

Spikenard (*Nardostachys jatamansi*) grows in cold
dry pastures of the Himalayas, and is brought from
there to the plains of India, where it forms a considerable article of commerce today even as it did in ancient
times.

It is a perennial herb of the Valerian family, related
to the common *Valeriana officinalis* of our gardens, but
with an even stronger and more pleasantly scented root.
The roots and young stems—before the leaves unfold
—are used to make the perfume.

SPICERY

Among the plants which may have contributed to
the spicery and spices of Genesis (*37:25*) and (*43:11*)
are two vetches known as *Astragalus gummifer* and
A. tragacantha. Plants of the Astragalus group prefer
light porous soils and no shade, and are propagated by
seed, although seed of the species named above is not

listed in American seed catalogues. An American relative of the Astragalus of the Bible is our native locoweed of the prairie (*A. mollissimus*).

STACTE

The stacte of the Bible verse, "Take unto thee sweet spices, stacte and onycha and galbanum" (*Ex. 30:34*), may be the sweet storax of the plant *Styrax officinalis*, a small tree or an irregularly stiff-branched shrub, abundant in Palestine. Its gum is highly perfumed, and is prized today as it probably was in ancient days.

Storax (*Styrax officinalis*) is a handsome shrub of graceful and spreading habit, with white, fragrant flowers. It is hardy only in the South. It is well adapted for borders of shrubberies, or as single specimens on the lawn, and thrives best in a light, porous soil. Propagation is by seed.

SWEET CANE

The Bible references to sweet cane do not give satisfactory clues to the identification of the plant. Jeremiah (*6:20*) says that it was from a far country. Some commentators believe that the sweet cane of the Bible may have been the plant which we know as sugar cane (*Saccharum officinarum*). This is an attractive plant for the garden although because it is an economic plant few gardeners think of it for the home garden. It is extremely ornamental and will make a striking specimen in any church garden. Sugar cane has been propagated by cuttings from time immemorial so that many varieties have lost the power to flower and set seed.

THYINE WOOD

Among the articles of merchandise of the fallen Babylon is thyine wood, of which so little is known that its identification is difficult (*Rev. 18:11-13*). It may have been the wood of a tree known as *Tetraclinis articulata,* or *Callitris quadrivalvis,* a conifer related to the arbor vitae and native to Algeria and other parts of the Atlas Mountains of Northern Africa. It seldom exceeds a height of thirty feet. The dark-colored, fragrant wood takes on a high polish and furnishes fine timber which, owing to its resinous properties, is little subject to decay, and remains uninjured by insects.

8

Reeds and Rushes

BESIDE running streams and especially in the margins of lakes and pools, in damp meadows and marshy places, grew the reeds, rushes and sedges of the Bible.

These plants were like palm trees in that they brought the good news of water in a thirsty land; Job says, "Can the rush grow up without mire?" (*Job 8:11*); and Isaiah observed that when rivers were emptied the reeds would wither (*Isa. 19:6, 7*).

Reeds and rushes growing in the desert would be evidence that the desert had disappeared, and this disappearance of the desert was, like that of the sea, a part of the prophetic vision of an expanding land. So Isaiah, speaking of the glorious day when God's blessings should fill the world, said that the desert would have water, and reeds and rushes would spring up beside the pools. This promise is in the short but eloquent thirty-fifth chapter, where we find, also, Isaiah's promise that the desert shall blossom as the rose, the blind shall see, the deaf shall hear, the dumb shall sing, and the ransomed of the Lord shall return.

In another sense, reeds were untrustworthy. They were used as walking-sticks, and to lean upon a staff of reed became a figure of speech based on this fact. If you leaned too heavily, such a thin staff might break and pierce your hand, or wrench your body. For a man or a nation to be a "broken reed," or a "bruised reed," became a common expression for weakness. Thus when Jesus wanted his audience to understand that he would be kind to those weak in body or in faith, he said, "A bruised reed shall he not break" (*Matt 12:20*).

In the historic prophecies, this delicate walking-stick, this staff of reed, became emblematic of Egypt, where the papyrus grew. The simile must have been startlingly effective at a time when the physical power of Egypt was so obvious that the temptation was great to covet Egyptian wealth, to trust in the material power of Egyptian horses and chariots and all weapons of war. Egypt was the old, the great, the often-victorious civilization. The little kingdoms of Israel and Judah were constantly leaning upon Egypt, hoping that she would protect them from the Assyrians or other conquerors that threatened or swept down. But over and over again Isaiah, Jeremiah and Ezekiel warned the people to put their trust in God, not in the temporal power that was a staff of reed, a bruised reed or a broken reed.

Thus, during the reign of Hezekiah in Judah, we find Egypt called a bruised reed. "Thou trusteth upon the staff of this bruised reed, even upon Egypt, on which if a man lean, it will go into his hand, and pierce it: so is Pharaoh king of Egypt unto all that trust on him" (*II Kings 18:21*). The parallel of these words, and an elaboration upon them are found in Isaiah. He told the people that their trust in the strength of Pharaoh would be their shame and confusion (*Isa. 30:1-5*). "Woe to them that go down to Egypt for help, and stay on horses, and trust in chariots . . . Now the

Egyptians are men, and not God; and their horses flesh, and not spirit" (*Isa. 31:1-3*). And again, in a verse which he lifts from Kings, "Lo, thou trusteth in the staff of this broken reed, on Egypt; whereon if a man lean, it will go into his hand, and pierce it; so is Pharaoh king of Egypt to all that trust in him" (*Isa. 36:6*).

Isaiah, as we can see, advocated confidence in the Lord, and the promotion of social and religious reforms at home, but too many people turned deaf ears upon his message. Judah became the vassal of first one conqueror and then another. Confidence in Egypt never saved her. Years later, Jeremiah and Ezekiel were still warning the people against Egypt. "Behold, Pharaoh's army, which is come forth to help you, shall return to Egypt into their own land" (*Jer. 37:7*). "And all the inhabitants of Egypt shall know that I am the Lord, because they have been a staff of reed to the house of Israel. When they took hold of thee by thy hand, thou didst break, and rend all their shoulder: and when they leaned upon thee, thou brakest, and madest all their loins to be at a stand" (*Eze. 29:6, 7*).

To follow the role played by the broken reed, Egypt, in the political history of Israel and Judah, will lead to a close study of the movements of the material history of those times, and how they were reflected in the spiritual messages of the prophets which lived through those turbulent times.

But there is a special connection between the reeds and rushes, and the Word of God as we have it in the Bible, for our word Bible comes from "biblos," the Greek word for papyrus, the bulrush from which paper was made.

Paper was made from rushes and written on, by the scribes, with a reed pen. These two plants are, therefore, the servants of the written word, sustaining it as wheat fed the people, and so worthy of the respect of all readers who reverence the Scriptures.

It is true that the books of the Bible, in their earliest form, were written on parchment or even leaves of plants which were used as paper, and not on papyrus. There seems to be no record of the use, by the people of Palestine, of papyrus for paper. But it was so used in Egypt, and Egyptian methods of paper making spread to Greece and Rome. Valuable documentary evidence of the life and customs of Bible times have come down to us in ancient papyri; original documents such as private letters, wills, contracts, complaints, petitions and invitations corroborate the canonical writings. In papyri unearthed by the archeologists, we meet at first hand the husbandman, the soldier, the publican, the householder in domestic relations, the steward and his accounts, the thief, the retired veteran, the money lender, and many other individuals referred to in the Old and New Testaments. Here we learn more of the social evils against which the prophets, and later Paul, spoke so sternly.

But it is less the original document than the distribution of the Scriptures to which paper and paper making, and the reed pen, contributed. Sacred writing might be graven on stone or written on expensive parchment, and be preserved. But for circulation among the people, some cheaper, easier, more practical method of copying had to be found, and this problem was solved by paper. The modern world followed the ancient world in its

use; and though other plants were found to furnish the
raw material, the process of paper making to which we
owe the Bible of Gutenberg and Wycliffe and King
James, the paper we use today and on which this book
is printed, goes back directly to the bulrushes growing
in the Nile mud and pressed into papyrus sheets by the
ingenious Egyptians. In this sense, the reed of Egypt
was never broken.

Among the reeds and rushes of the Bible were plants
that are world-wide in their distribution. Our common
American cattails, so much at home in our own swampy
lands, were equally at home in Bible lands. But among
all the grasses and sedges that grew at the water's edge,
the most conspicuous and ornamental were those known
to us as Giant Reed and as Papyrus. These plants are
not native to our country but have been introduced here,
and are great favorites with all gardeners.

BULRUSHES

Papyrus, known to us as the plant which furnished
paper for the ancients, is sometimes called bulrushes,
sometimes flags, reeds and rushes in the Bible. This
plant is associated in our minds with the story of the
baby Moses as the material of the little ark in which he
was set afloat, and as the plant which grew in profusion
at the water's edge where he was hidden.

In chapter one of Exodus we read that a new king
arose over Egypt, one who knew not Joseph, and he said
unto his people:

"Behold, the people of the children of Israel are
more and mightier than we."

Pharaoh, therefore, decided to "deal wisely" with them. He put them to work bearing burdens, building for him the treasure cities of Pithom and Raamses. The Egyptians made the lives of the Israelites "bitter with hard bondage, in mortar and in brick and in all manner of service in the field." But still the Israelites multiplied and grew strong, so that Pharaoh decided that every son born to an Israelite family should be cast into the river and destroyed. It was from this fate that the mother of Moses wanted to save her son. When he was three months old, and she could no longer keep him concealed in her own home, she built an ark of bulrushes, daubed it with slime and pitch, and hid him in the jungle of papyrus and other plants that grew in the shallow waters of the Nile where it was the habit of Pharaoh's daughter to take her daily bath. And when Pharaoh's daughter found the child, she adopted him, and he grew up in the house of the king.

Papyrus (*Cyperus papyrus* or *Papyrus antiquorum*) flourished along the banks of the Nile in Bible times but today has disappeared almost entirely from Egypt. It still grows in swampy places in Palestine, but not in profusion.

Papyrus, as paper, is depicted on the earliest monuments in the shape of a long rectangular sheet, rolled up at one end. The remains of many such rolled sheets have been found in Egyptian tombs. The scribe wrote upon this roll with a reed, and his black and red ink was made of animal carbon.

The paper, itself, was made from the pith of the plant which was taken from the thick portion of the stem. The thick lower part of the stem which was in the mud and water contained the whitish and most compact part of the pith. The outer stem was peeled off, and the inner pith was cut into thin slices which were placed side by side with their edges overlapping one another, and crosswise upon this sheet were placed one or more sheets, then the whole was sprinkled with gummy water and subjected to pressure, and then left to dry in the sun.

The width of the sheets depended upon the length of the papyrus stems taken, but they could be made any length by joining a number of sections end to end. The scapus, or roll, usually consisted of about twenty sections joined together. When newly prepared, the paper was white or of tannish color and pliable; but those which have been unearthed in modern times have become dark brown and brittle so that they break to the touch.

In olden times, papyrus had many uses besides that of paper. It was made into crowns for the head, into sandals, boxes and boats. The pith was boiled and eaten; and the root, when dried, was used for fuel.

The papyrus plant has a three-sided stem which attains a height of from eight to sixteen feet, with a thickness of two or three inches at the base. The stem tapers upward gradually and ends in a sheath from which issues a large tuft of grasslike panicles, bearing numerous florets like grass. It is handsome to look at, and the large, fluffy heads make attractive interior decorations.

Its graceful and ornamental form has long been in demand for water gardens in this country. When planted in a tub or box of rich soil and placed in an artificial pond, the tops of the fleshy rootstocks should protrude out of the water. It is not hardy in the North, but the shorter stems can be lifted with part of the rootstock and grown as a house plant in winter. It can be propagated by seed, sown in early autumn or spring, and by division of the large plants in spring.

REEDS

The giant reed (*Arundo donax*) is certainly one of the reeds of various references in the Scriptures, although the common cat-tail, and the sorghum may also be included.

The giant reed grows to a height of from eight to ten feet and forms impenetrable thickets in the Jordan Valley in some places on the margins of the Dead Sea. Its stem has a diameter of two or three inches at the base, terminated by a beautiful and massive plume of flowers similar to that of sugar-cane and pampas grass. It was a beautiful, fresh green in summer when all else was dead and dry, and of fine appearance in full bloom when the silky panicles crowned the top of every reed.

The "covert of the reed" (*Job 40:21*) sheltered animal and bird life, and the thriving appearance of this reed in the dry season must have influenced Isaiah to include the mention of "reeds and rushes" in his thirty-fifth chapter, as one of the beauties of the day of restoration. It was used for many purposes by the ancients —walking sticks, fishing rods, measuring rods, and musical pipes, so that grown in the Bible garden, it can become the starting point for the long and interesting study of the history of Israel and Judah and the broken reed.

This reed may also lead us to a further study of Ezekiel and his glorious vision of the Temple, and the corresponding passages about the Temple and the Holy City in Revelation. A man appears with a measuring reed (*Eze. 40:3* and *42:16*) to measure the Temple which, to Ezekiel, signified that the people would turn from all their old idolatries to the worship and love of the one God. The Temple seems to represent a glorious spiritual reconstruction, and the man with a measuring rod is there to note its perfect symmetry and harmony so that the symmetry and harmony of God shall nevermore be lost or forgotten. We read: "And there was given me a reed like unto a rod: and the angel stood, saying, Rise, and measure the temple of God, and the altar, and them that worship therein" (*Rev. 11:1*).

And again, in Revelation, the Holy City is measured with a golden reed: "And he that talked with me had a golden reed to measure the city, and the gates thereof, and the wall thereof. And the city lieth foursquare, and the length is as large as the breadth: and he measured the city with the reed . . ." (*Rev. 21:15, 16*).

The giant reed is a tall reedlike grass with broad flat blades and lovely terminal panicles; it has large knotty rootstocks, and grows often as a lawn plant in Western and Southern gardens. It should be protected in the North.

The cat-tail (*Typa latifolia*) is easily grown in a pool or in any spot in the garden that can be kept moist, such as near a dripping water faucet. It will spread through its creeping rootstocks but not beyond the point where there is moisture. Its narrow, flat leaves and odd, brown flowers in dense, blunt spikes are decorative, and the plant has a stately effect in the garden. It can be propagated by seeds planted in pots kept in water.

The sorghum (*Holcus sorghum*) is thought by some commentators to have been the reed used to lift the vinegar sponge to Jesus when he was on the cross. The verse describing this act appears in three places. In Matthew (*27:48*) and in Mark (*15:36*) the sponge is described as having been lifted on a reed; in John (*19:29*) the sponge is put upon a hyssop, which has already been noticed in the section on hyssop in a previous chapter, *A Garden of Herbs*.

RUSHES

Among the ancients, "palm-branch and rush" was an expression which stood for the "highest and lowest," the lofty and most humble. Isaiah used this expression to signify that God would punish the great and small; that he would punish all classes of society for their sins. "The Lord will cut off from Israel head and tail, branch and rush, in one day" (*Isa. 9:14*). And again, "Neither shall there be any work for Egypt, which the head or tail, branch or rush, may do" (*Isa. 19:15*). For the day will come when all Egypt shall be afraid of the shaking of God's hand, and Judah's God shall be a terror unto Egypt.

The rush probably refers to any number of the species of *Scirpus* and *Juncus* that grew in the East, many of these plants being world wide in their distribution. The plants of the *Scirpus* genus are members of the Sedge family, a large group of rushlike or grasslike plants inhabiting the whole globe. One of the particular species is known to us today as the Great Bulrush (*Scirpus lacustris*); it has a height of from three to nine feet, and is apparently leafless, making a mass of spikes terminating in dense clusters. Another species (*Scirpus holochoemus*) is stiff and rushlike, with a few narrow leaves and dense heads of spikelets.

The plants of the genus *Juncus* are stiff, perennial herbs, resembling grasses. They grow in wet places and have unbranched, round stems. The leaves are narrow and flat, like grass leaves, and they bear small clusters of greenish or brownish flowers.

The plant known to us as the common rush is *Juncus effusus*. It has a soft stem and grows to a height of four feet. It was one of the rushes of the Bible and is widely distributed in the north temperate zone.

Papyrus—celebrated as the source of the first paper—is the bulrush of Scriptures.

This beautiful Holy Thistle, well known in America, is a typical Bible weed. A field overgrown with thorns and thistles became a proverbial sign of the slothful farmer.

9

Thorns and Thistles

ARMORED plants—defending themselves with prickles, thorns and stinging hairs—are characteristic of dry environments the world over. Palestine
seemed to have more than her share. Not only were the
weeds of the country prickly and stinging, but many of
the choicest trees and shrubs produced their quota of
thorns. The acacia, so valuable in the desert as the chief
source of wood, had thorns, as did also the lovely oleaster, or oil tree, which grew in Palestine proper and
which decorates the American landscape under the name
of Russian olive.

The modern traveler, viewing the thorns and thistles
of Palestine, comes away with the idea that the American prickly pear is the most characteristic weed of the
Holy Land. Not only has the American cactus invaded
Jerusalem since the discovery of the New World, but
many other thorny plants have traveled there in fairly
modern times, so that botanists have had difficulty in
learning just which ones were the annoying thorns and
thistles that provide symbols for all that is unpleasant,
undesirable and evil in the Bible.

But we know definitely that many unfriendly, thorny
plants were present in those times. It was not easy for
the wayfarer in Bible days to escape the prick of the
thorn or the sting of the nettle as he walked through

the countryside. Paul's "thorn in the flesh" is the perfect simile for an ill as nagging as a thorn to a man who counted it part of his work to walk for many miles through thorny thickets or over stony roads where the only shade would be that of a thorny shrub. The pricking brier and grieving thorn were common expressions used early in Old Testament days, and heathen peoples are described as "pricks in your eyes" and "thorns in your sides" (*Numb. 33:55* and *Judges 2:3*). The threat to tear the flesh with thorns and briers occurs in Judges (*8:7*), while briers and thorns and scorpions were figures of speech that made graphic the opposition in the path of Ezekiel's spiritual teaching (*2:6*).

While thorns and brambles tore the flesh and obstructed the path of the wayfarer, they were welcomed as a source of fuel for the campfire. The dry, brittle plants caught on fire easily and burned quickly, but even as firewood they left much to be desired, a fact which gave rise to the familiar comparison of foolish laughter to "the crackling of thorns under a pot," a sound soon ended (*Eccl. 7:6*). The thorn fire might flare quickly, but before it could give useful heat, the fire would be scattered by the wind (*Ps. 58:9*). On the other hand, while the thorn may have been a convenience to the wayfarer as fuel, however inadequate its heat, it was a distinct fire hazard to the rest of the vegetation of the land—to cultivated crops, to pasture grassland and to forest. In Exodus (*22:6*), the law for restitution of accidental damage to another's property mentions the fire which starts in thorns and spreads to a cornfield. The thorns are always the first to burn, and a dreaded forest fire starts in brush. The fire "shall devour the briers and thorns, and shall kindle in the thickets of the forests" (*Isa. 9:18*). It is a description that is true of forest fires today.

The bramble, a plant to be scorned for its worthlessness when compared to the fruitful olive and vine, becomes the symbol of the unworthy man who would set himself up as king. Jotham's fable of how the trees chose a king, surely a model for Aesop, not only delights us for its satiric quality, but leads us back to the early days of the Judges to study again the evolution of the idea of kingship among the Israelites. Gideon has become the hero of the moment, and the people invite him to become king (*Judges 8:22, 23; 9:8-15*).

"Rule thou over us, both thou, and thy son, and thy son's son also: for thou hast delivered us from the hand of Midian," the men of Israel said to Gideon.

"I will not rule over you, neither shall my son rule over you," was Gideon's answer. "The Lord shall rule over you."

When Gideon died, however, his illegitimate son, Abimelech, decided to take advantage of this longing of the people for a king. He set himself up as the royal leader of the people and in the midst of the royal celebration, Jotham, who held Gideon's belief that only the Lord should rule His people, lifted up his voice, delivering this biting satire to all who might listen:

"Reign thou over us," said all the trees to the olive. But that valuable working tree, producer of the golden oil that was the fat of the land and the light of the Temple, was far too wise to feel tempted by such an empty honor.

"Should I leave my fatness," said the olive, "wherewith by me they honor God and man, and go to be promoted over the trees?"

Next they chose the fig tree, but the fertile fig said scornfully:

"Should I forsake my sweetness, and my good fruit, and go to be promoted over the trees?"

Then said the trees unto the vine, "Come thou, and reign over us." But the vine declined as firmly:

"Should I leave my wine, which cheereth God and man, and go to be promoted over the trees?"

Then said all the trees to the bramble, "Come *thou,* and reign over us." And the bramble, crooked but willing to climb, said:

"If in truth ye anoint me king over you, then come and put your trust in my shadow." This was a nice touch of sarcasm, since the shadow of the bramble certainly made no shade. And adding a boastful threat to sarcasm, the bramble continued, "If not, let fire come out of the bramble, and devour the cedars of Lebanon!"

Although thorns and thistles, brambles, briers and nettles seem far removed from the grandeur of the cedar, from the fruitfulness of the olive, vine and fig, they have their place in the large economy of nature. But if we accept the definition of a weed as that of a plant out of place, then the prickly plants that invaded the fields of Palestine were weeds of the worst description. They were enemies against which the more tender, cultivated plants, useful to man, could not contend. The wheat, growing among thorns, was sure to be choked sooner or later by the latter's rank growth. So Jesus, in his parable of the sower, explained that the words of the gospel were choked by the "care of this world and the deceitfulness of riches" (*Matt. 13:22*), just as the sower's seeds that fell among thorns were choked and unable to mature and become fruitful.

The man who tilled the soil, if he was a careful husbandman, had constantly to be on guard against weeds, a condition which is as true of farmers today as in Bible times. Then as now, the good land yielded its fatness to those who worked for it, and the field overgrown with thorns or thistles became a proverbial sign of the slothful farmer (*Prov. 24:30-31*), and symbolized the man whose mind and heart were in similar condition:

> I went by the field of the slothful,
> And by the vineyard of the man void of understanding;
> And, lo, it was all grown over with thorns,
> And nettles had covered the face thereof,
> And the stone wall thereof was broken down.

This growth of undesirable plants as a result of man's neglect of the land, attributable to human mismanagement rather than to the planning of Providence, is forecast in Genesis. There, in the account of Eden there is no mention of nuisance plants—all the first growth of the Garden is either "pleasant to the eye" or "good for food." But after Adam's transgression, it is part of the payment that the ground shall bring forth thorns and thistles (*Gen. 3:18*).

The contrast between the well cultivated, fruitful fields and abandoned land that had been conquered by weeds was an image of which the prophets made eloquent use in rebuking a wicked and disobedient people. Seers and prophets did not lack that spiritual vision which enabled them to place first the loss of higher

values, but they sought, and found, words to appeal directly to their audiences. To tell a man that his sins
would be as a hedge of thorns across his path (*Prov.
15:19* and *Hosea 2:6*) was to speak in terms he could
not fail to understand.

Isaiah (*5:2-9*) described the vineyard of the Lord
which brought forth wild grapes as fit only to be over-
come by briers and thorns, and he made it plain that
briers and thorns represented the enemies of Israel and
Judah who were going to overrun vineyards, fields and
even the cities if the people did not repent. His unfor-
gettable picture of desolation includes "thorns . . . in
her palaces, nettles and brambles in the fortresses thereof: and it shall be an habitation of dragons, and a court
for owls" (*Isa. 34:13*).

Hosea prophesies (*9:6 and 10:8*) that the thorn and
thistle shall come up on the altars, that nettles and
thorns shall possess the tabernacles, if the sinful people
persist in sin. It was not long before these Old Testament prophecies came true in part; and in the years that
followed, on through the Middle Ages and down to
modern times, the prophecies of desolation became
etched, deeper and deeper, into the face of the land.
For when the land which once flowed with milk and
honey became the pawn of nations, care of the soil was
neglected.

The Hebrews of Bible days had respected the land
and its fertile soil as blessings of God that must be protected and guarded from destruction, as man's own
moral nature was to be carefully cultivated and guarded
from forces that would destroy. Beyond the almost
mystic identification of land and people already noted,

there was the practical fact that a man's attitude towards the land, the common heritage, was an index of his moral responsibility.

Never more surely than in agriculture could rewards and punishments be more clearly assessed in moral terms, and throughout the Old Testament judgments are frequent against the man who neglects the land. "The whole land is made desolate," says Jeremiah, "because no man layeth it to heart . . . They have sown wheat, but shall reap thorns" (*Jer. 12:11, 13*). While Job, to justify his own righteousness, hastens to say that he has been a good farmer:

> If my land cry out against me,
> And the furrows thereof weep together . . .
>
> Let thistles grow instead of wheat,
> And cockles instead of barley.

Work on the land was not merely to make crops for immediate benefit, but to preserve and improve the soil. Hillsides subject to the wash of rain and the force of wind were constantly protected; only the man "void of understanding" permitted his vineyard walls to go untended. Ancient methods of terracing for vine culture were so perfectly adapted to protecting the hillsides that it was many years before modern growers realized that the wine grape could be grown in any other way.

The Bible is full of references to the gathering of stones to make walls for the hillside vineyards. We can see today, in Palestine, the remains of this elaborate terrace system, and modern experts say that terraces such as those of Bible times, if built and paid for in modern money, would cost from two to three thousand dollars an acre. But vine growers of ancient days so valued the soil that they willingly spent the equivalent in hard work. God had given the land; productivity of its soil was the source of wealth for the people. Those who appreciated the inheritance would work to keep it.

It is not known whether the ancient woodcutters practiced a system of controlled cutting of the forest, but even with the tremendous demand made by Solomon for the building of the Temple, the forests were not destroyed. The "glory of Lebanon" was appreciated not only for the beauty of the trees and the usefulness of the timber, but as a source of the nation's water supply. References to the streams from Lebanon, the springs and fountains which sprang from the foot of the mountains, speak of "living waters." This phrase, symbolic of the Holy Spirit, is true also when considered in terms of weather and climate; it is a poet's expression of a fact well known to modern conservationists. The forests caught the rainfall and melting snows, the roots of the trees were reservoirs to hold the water, which was released in streams, springs and fountains to provide the means of life during the dry season.

Today it is easy for us to see that the modern scientist and the Bible seer and prophet really meet on common ground as far as the land is concerned. The only difference is that modern man expresses himself in the language of science while the prophet spoke in the language of the poet. Both recognize the laws of the good earth and the need for conservation which forbids waste and greed. Both recognize that there is an inner order and harmony in nature, as in man, which requires only the well intentioned and intelligent working of men with each other and with the earth to prove once more that the earth is the Lord's and the fullness thereof; that the trees shall yield their fruit; that the rain from heaven need not fail; that deserts and dustbowls can blossom like the rose.

Today we talk of the cycle of plant life, and recognize a succession which may begin with lichens and mosses but ends with the flourishing of magnificent trees. Isaiah saw the same natural cycle, and described the glorious day when the earth should bud and give bread. In that day, when the mountains and hills shall break forth into singing and all the trees of the field shall clap their hands, "instead of the thorn shall come up the fir tree, and instead of the brier shall come up the myrtle tree" (*Isa. 55:13*).

Visitors to Palestine in modern times saw a land so unlike the glowing picture described in the Bible that they came away shocked and disappointed. Some few read in the scene the work of the blundering hand of man, others explained the barren rocky waste as a result of a "change in climate." And change in climate there has been, but a change such as that wrought by man when he removes trees and grass, where formerly they were meant to grow; the same kind of change which we have brought about in sections of our own American continent.

It was to this country, desolated not by inevitable climatic changes but by the mistakes of men, that the builders of a new Zion went back in recent years. By using modern methods of irrigation, with back breaking toil and with stout, courageous hearts, the modern citi-

zens of Palestine undertook to prove that the land of
the Bible was still a land of milk and honey. In many
sections they have planted orchards which yield a rich
harvest of fruit, for—like the American Southwest,
which it resembles in so many ways—Palestine responds
to irrigation. The land is slowly being brought back,
but this will be the work of centuries; soil in which to
grow crops and trees is accumulated slowly, as our own
American agronomists have pointed out many times.

The difficulty of restoring the land of Palestine in the
twentieth century is that the country is still in the path
of larger and more warlike nations. The people who
till the soil must now, as before, fight human enemies,
until the time shall come that Micah promised—the day
when nations shall beat swords into plowshares, spears
into pruninghooks, and cease to learn war; "but they
shall sit every man under his vine and under his fig tree,
and none shall make them afraid."

ACANTHUS

The name acanthus does not appear in the Bible,
neither do many other names under which the plants are
listed in this chapter. Although seventeen different Hebrew words were used for plants with prickles and
thorns, none of them corresponds to specific modern
names of plants. Neither etymologists nor botanists have
been able to unravel the tangle of names, and to identify
the thorns and thistles and other weeds of Bible times
by comparing them with the plants that are present
today in the Holy Land, often leads to even more confusion. The plants which are listed here, however, are

certain to have been present in Bible times, because they are known to have been native to the region or to have traveled there in ancient times. Except for a few, they are not the choicest of garden plants, and some plants are merely listed for the sake of the students and botanists who are interested in plants as botanical species.

The acanthus, more familiarly known as Bear's Breech (*Acanthus spinosa* and *A. syriacus*), is a perennial thistlelike herb or small shrub about three feet tall. It does best in rich, well drained soil and full sunlight, and is especially useful for background plantings. Although semihardy it needs heavy winter protection in the North. Propagation is by division of roots which may be done in spring or early autumn, and by seeds sown in April. The flowers, dull white to rose or purplish, and densely clustered, bloom in August.

Students of architecture recognize the curly acanthus leaf as a familiar design, used most effectively on the elaborately carved Corinthian column, and suggesting the love of ornament which Paul found it necessary to reprove.

BUCKTHORN

The buckthorns are handsome ornamental plants with attractive foliage, sometimes growing to the height of small trees. The large leaves are bright green and the flowers, an inconspicuous, greenish cluster, are followed by berrylike—usually black, but sometimes red—fruit. They are useful in planting in shrubberies and some are popular as hedge plants. The species of the Bible is given by the botanists as *Rhamnus palaestina*.

BRAMBLE

Among the brambles and briers of the Scriptures were undoubtedly the species *Rubus sanctus* and *R. ulmifolius*. The latter is sometimes cultivated in this country for its evergreen foliage and double red or pink flowers. The stems are curved, prostrate, and covered with stout prickles.

CHARLOCK

Charlock or wild mustard (*Brassica arvensis* or *Sinapis arvensis*) is a notorious weed of the Holy Land, and the botanists believe that it was well represented there in Bible days.

CHRIST'S THORN

Christ's thorn, or Jerusalem thorn (*Paliurus Spina-Christi*), is believed by most commentators to have been the plant from which Christ's crown of thorns was made. The jujube (*Zizyphus Spina-Christi*) is also suggested as the plant of the crown of thorns. All authorities are agreed, however, that the plant called "Crown of Thorns" (*Euphorbia splendens*) was not connected with Christ in any way, since this plant is a native of Madagascar and had not traveled to Palestine in ancient times.

Christ's thorn is a spreading, spiny shrub or small tree, sometimes procumbent, sometimes growing to a height of twenty feet. The fruit is brownish yellow and shiny; the foliage is dark green. It grows in well drained soil and prefers a sunny and warm position. It is not reliably hardy north of Washington, D. C.

CORN COCKLE

The corn cockle (*Agrostemma githago* and *Lychnis githago*) is common in fields of Palestine; it is a strong growing and very troublesome weed in grain fields.

DARNEL GRASS

This is a weed, resembling wheat, and called "tares" which grew in the cultivated fields of Palestine. (See section on wheat in Chapter 6.)

HOARY NIGHTSHADE

The hoary nightshade (*Solanum incanum*), a relative of the potato, is a common weed in Palestine and Egypt. Its berries resemble grapes in form, although they are narcotic and poisonous.

Two other nightshades (*Solanum sodomeum* and *S. sanctum*) are also among the weeds of the Bible. *Solanum sodomeum* is a coarse stiff-branched shrub, its branches and leaves armed with reddish spines. It grows to a height of from four to five feet, has flowers very much like those of a potato, and fruit about the size of an apple, which is handsomely yellow when ripe. The fruit is, at first, pulp inside, but as it ripens this pulp dries up, and on being pressed, bursts and emits a cloud of "dust and ashes."

HOLY THISTLE

The holy thistle (*Silybum marianum*) is also known as St. Mary's thistle, milk thistle and blessed thistle. It is an annual, biennial or perennial herb, growing to a height of four feet and sometimes much higher. It has spiny, glossy leaves and rose-purple flower heads surrounded by spiny bracts. It is naturalized in California where it has become a weed in the fields, but in the garden it is a particularly handsome plant when young. Its flower heads, with their decorative spines, make excellent subjects for flower arrangement groups both in the fresh and the dried form.

JUJUBE

The jujube (*Zizyphus Spina-Christi* and *Z. vulgaris*) have been identified by some commentators as the crown of thorns of the crucified Savior. Whether it was the plant of the crown is open to question, but it was undoubtedly one of the thorns of the Bible, since it grows in the Holy Land. *Z. vulgaris* is a spiny, middle-sized tree, averaging about twenty-five feet in height and covered with rough, brown bark. It has many branches covered with thorns. The small flowers are pale yellow and solitary. Its edible fruit is berrylike, with a two-seeded nut at its center. The fleshy exterior is saffron colored when ripe and has the form and size of a ripe olive.

It is not hardy north of Washington, D. C., but its handsome foliage makes it attractive for planting in shrubberies. The seeds should be cracked before planting, otherwise it will take them a couple of years to germinate.

NETTLES

There are a number of true nettles in the Holy Land, and the following species are named as representing the nettles of the Bible: *Urtica dioica, U. pilulifera, U. urene* and *U. membranacea.*

STAR THISTLE

The star thistle (*Centaurea calcitrapa* and *C. verutum*) has flowers of pale, purplish rose. On the flower heads are long, sharp spines. The plant is dull green, somewhat hairy; it blooms in July. The dried plants can be used effectively in combination with other plants in flower arrangements.

10

To Everything There Is a Season

A TIME to plant, and a time to pluck up that which is planted; a time to every purpose under heaven, says the Scriptures. And so, a time has come to speak of special plans for a Bible garden, of special ways in which Bible flowers and fruits can be used, and of suggestions for study projects based on an interest in Bible plants. For the making of Bible gardens, either at home or in the church yard, is an undertaking upon which old and young can cooperate. All can enjoy the garden together, for it will be a delightful spot during summer where entertainments, weddings, and evening services can be held. The church garden is one more way of bringing the church into the daily lives of its people, for the garden can be used every day in the week, not only when the congregation gathers there in the name of the Lord, but by those who seek, in moments of solitude, a place to rest and meditate.

The Bible garden will be one of living walls of green, enclosing the lawn and its flower borders, and perhaps a pool or fountain; creating a scene of beauty in which one may find peace and rebirth of spirit, a place where a man and his neighbor can gather, literally, under his own vine and fig tree and be unafraid. From the Bible garden you may pluck flowers and foliage to be used indoors in arrangements that will revive cherished Bible associations; and when carried to the sick these flowers of faith will offer their silent prayer of hope and cheer.

In planning the garden for home or church, the Cedar of Lebanon, which thrives in such opposite climates as California and Massachusetts, will be first choice among the trees. Planted in the Bible garden, this cedar will display the same magnificence and grandeur which so impressed the Bible poets and prophets. To study next Sunday's Bible lesson in the shade of this noble tree, to gather beneath its protecting branches for a summer sermon at the church, will be to experience that renewed confidence and security which always come when we are able to establish new means of contact with the Bible.

If your property is not large enough to accommodate the spreading, horizontal branches of the cedar, there are many other Bible trees from which you may choose. The white poplar which grows to a height of ninety feet; the Oriental plane which grows to a height of eighty feet, or in the hybrid form, to one hundred feet; the crack or brittle willow, which attains a height from fifty to sixty feet; the trembling aspen, of similar height; and the Persian walnut, which grows to seventy feet— all are perfectly at home in this country, and are easily obtainable and easily grown. In the South and West, you have a larger choice of trees for there you can also grow the luxuriant carob, the holm oak, the pistacia, the terebinth, the Italian cypress and the date palm. On smaller properties, a fruit tree such as the apricot, which in some varieties grows into a sizable tree, may become the principal tree of a Bible garden. The apricot grows in the East and West.

For the hedge, the shrubbery border or the screen

that encloses the property as a whole, or which may enclose special areas within it, there is a choice of excellent
material. The box, oleaster, savin and common juniper;
figs, quinces, small varieties of apricot and almond; and
the fast-growing luxuriant-leaved, annual castor bean,
offer a choice from which to make a beautiful and satisfactory planting in the Northeastern States. Figs, apricots and almonds are hardy in the Northeast if planted
in protected positions. Going south, other plants may be
added to the shrubbery border or hedge; the pomegranate, hardy as far north as Washington, D. C., the profusely blooming oleander, the fragrant flowered myrtle,
the aromatic sweet bay, and in the Southwest the olive
and palm can become important as tree or shrub.

The grapevine will be an important part of the plan
of every Bible garden, although, as has been pointed
out before, gardeners in the East may have to compro-
mise and cover the arbor or trellis with a native or
hybrid grape rather than with the true Bible species.
The vine may grow on a pergola extending from the
house over the terrace, and the lawn adjoining the terrace may be enclosed with Bible shrubs, and the flower
border placed between lawn and shrubbery walls.

In another location, the entrance to the Bible garden
may be through a vine-covered arch in the arbor. This
entrance will lead directly to an enclosure formed by
the arbor on one side and hedges, shrubs or walls on the
other sides. The flower garden may be in the form of
borders surrounding a rectangle of grass or brick. A
large shrub or small shade tree, planted in the boundary
of this enclosure, will provide shade for chairs in which
to lounge and rest. The planting of the borders should

follow the usual plan of tall plants at the rear, low-growing plants in front. Small fruit trees, in tubs, may be sunk in the ground toward the back of the border nearest the hedge or wall. A choice of flax, love-in-a mist, larkspur, peony, lupine, pheasant's eye, Persian buttercup, violet and other "flowers of the field" will make the border gay with bloom. Anemones, narcissi and hyacinths may be placed so that the space later left by their dying foliage will be well concealed by the green growth of annual flowers and herbs. The anemones should, of course, be the most conspicuous part of the planting if you live in the West or South, where it is possible to have a long season of bloom and where such a display demands little effort. In the East and North, anemones will flourish and bloom, but the season is confined to early spring. Mint, rue, dill, coriander, marjoram and other herbs are effective also in the flower border.

If the Bible garden is to be a formal one, then a pool or fountain may be placed so that it is reached by a cruciform arrangement of paths, the design of the cross being particularly appropriate for this type of garden.

Although a complete Bible garden will be certain to repay the effort required to plan and plant it, such an undertaking is not the only way to enjoy Bible plants. If the home or church garden is already well-established, you might plant a few Bible shrubs or flowers to blend with the landscape plan already under way. Once recognized as Bible plants, the fig, the apricot, box or castor bean, will cast a new light over the garden, giving it a spiritual glow which, though always present, may not have been so keenly appreciated before. The presence of a few Bible plants near the spot used as altar or pulpit when services and weddings are held out of doors will bring to the occasion new Biblical associations as well as beauty.

An ideal Bible garden for home or church may be raised in pots and tubs. Tubbed fig, pomegranate, oleander, apricot, almond, myrtle, sweet bay, castor bean, quince, olive, palm, juniper, box and oleaster can be placed on the flagstone terrace, in the courtyard, or on the lawn near the shrubbery or pool. A grouping of these tubbed plants will blend nicely with the scheme of the garden as a whole, and yet retain its own individuality as a special garden. Its great advantage, particularly for the church, is that it is movable and therefore may be arranged to suit the occasion and the crowd. Then, too, tubbed plants are a great advantage in the North, because the tubs can be moved to protected and sheltered positions during the winter, while tender plants such as oleanders and figs, can be stored in the cellar during their winter period of rest. Church members, no doubt, can accommodate other tubbed plants in their own greenhouses or on cool, glassed porches. The size of plants, grown in tubs, is automatically checked from growing too tall, so that a large collection of Bible plants can be used and enjoyed without having to give the whole garden over to them.

Another special advantage of the tub garden is that it reproduces the atmosphere of the Bible country. Such gardens are common today in the American Southwest, the part of our country in which we find obvious physical resemblances to Palestine; and we have reason to believe that in Bible times as now, the courtyards and flat rooftops of Oriental cities were filled with plants in pottery jars, tubs and baskets, much as are the patio gardens of our Southwest. If your only gardening space is the top of a city apartment house, you can still grow tubbed plants that will remind you of ancient roofs and courts where men sat by night to talk of the law of the Lord.

It is not only in the Bible garden, however, that you can enjoy Bible plants. You can bring a few flowers and foliage branches indoors, where they may contribute a sense of spiritual peace and refreshment to any and all rooms of the house. Let a few Bible flowers say silent grace at the dinner table, or permit them to serve as a text on any occasion of religious meaning. Build a Biblical idea into a simple plant and flower arrangement. Aaron's Rod, a branch of flowering almond, symbolic of the fulfillment of God's promise to man, may be placed on the table or desk beside the Bible. An olive branch, placed in a vase between candlesticks, may be symbolic of the olive which furnished the oil for the light of the Temple; or a drooping spray of olive upon which a pottery dove has been placed may represent the age-old emblem of peace.

Sprays of pomegranates, with their bell-like flowers, which furnished the design on priestly robes, and the design for bells in general, might be arranged on the table near a bell-like ornament, commemorating the use of church bells through the ages. The white, bunch-flowered narcissus, with white candles, and a figurine of a saint or madonna in white, can make an arrangement symbolic of innocence and purity.

Anemones, available perhaps from plants which you have forced for winter bloom, and always available

from florists during the winter months, may be arranged
in a vase for pulpit or home, a constant reminder of the
beauty of the scene in which Jesus stood as He delivered
the Sermon on the Mount. A vase of anemones, placed
beside a painting or image of Christ will be beautifully
appropriate, since these same flowers surrounded Jesus
in life.

Wheat, vine, fig and pomegranate may be combined
to symbolize the Land of Promise described in Deuter-
onomy, and an arrangement of wheat, grapevine and
olive can become the living emblem of the phrase "corn,
wine, and oil," which was the blessing of God upon
His children. The vine and fig together can become an
arrangement which means universal peace, and the
leaves and fruits of both vine and fig will make an excellent centerpiece for the family dinner table, where
it will be a symbol of domestic peace, prosperity and
happiness. The sickle, often mentioned in the Bible in
connection with the gathering of the harvest and the
vintage, can become an ornament to be combined with
sheaves of wheat and rich clusters of grapes.

An effective arrangement, in lighter tone, is that of
castor bean leaves—each a different size and different
color as they are at different stages of growth. The
leaves, in a container, placed beside a crystal fish, with
broad jaws and flipping tail, is a reminder of Jonah's
gourd and Jonah's whale. Other animals of the Bible
may also be used in combination with plants. The lamb,
the turtle dove, the deer will symbolize gentleness, or
speak of spring, as they do in the Song of Solomon. The
eagle and the lion symbolize strength in the Bible, and
both are associated with strong trees, such as the Cedar

of Lebanon. Ezekiel's parable of the eagle and the vine
(*17:1-10*) can become the subject of an arrangement.

Papyrus, reeds and water-lilies, arranged together,
beside which is placed an ornamental crocodile, will be
symbolic of the Egypt of Moses, and of the prophets,
who warned the Israelites against that broken reed, the
land of the crocodile, as a military ally.

A few sprays of leaves of the date palm, rising from
a flat bowl of sand, make an interesting table piece for
living room or nursery. For the children's table, the container of sand might be quite large, with a mirror buried
in it to represent the pool of water, and a camel standing nearby. As a project on which the children themselves could work, the bowl can be transformed into the
oasis of Elim, the Sacred Tree Oasis, where there were
three score and ten palm trees and twelve wells of water.
Here, after days of terrible thirst, the Children of
Israel and their herds and flocks were able to drink at
last. In building this scene, there should be tents which
the Israelites pitched at their camp, and sheep and goats,
but no camels.

For church supper and bazaar, Bible plant products
can be eaten, sold for profit and used for decorations.
Mint punch, pomegranate punch and watermelon punch
are all delightful party drinks. Watermelon punch can
be served, using a scooped-out watermelon as a punch
bowl. Beans or lentils and wheat bread might make the
most filling portion of the Bible plant meal, but salads
of mixed fruit, stuffed dates, or skinned grapes, topped
off with a dessert of apricot whip or pie, would be making
a most delectable use of Bible fruits. Place cards decorated with drawings of Bible plants, or small paper

plants used as favors, will add to the interest, while the table decorations would certainly be of arrangements of Bible fruits, leaves or flowers. Hothouse grapes and crimson pomegranates, dried wheat and sorghum heads, dried thistle heads, branches of dried thorn, sprays of evergreen from Bible trees and shrubs will be attractive for the fall and Thanksgiving table.

At other times, table decorations can be of fruits or leaves according to season. Vine leaves, fig leaves and castor bean leaves make excellent decorations either in vertical or horizontal arrangements, and when placed flat on the table, make a charming background for Bible fruits and vegetables. Remember that cucumbers are available all year round, and that even onions and leeks can be effective in decoration if the occasion is informal and rustic enough. Onions, lentils in the pod, leeks, cucumbers, wheat, sorghum, and sugar cane can be combined in many ingenious ways. Almonds, walnuts, pistachio nuts, dried carob beans are available all year round, and almonds in their green, fleshy coats are sold in the markets in early summer. Branches of these trees, with the almost ripe nuts still clinging to them, can be used as attractive decorations where the trees are available in abundance. Even watermelons, though large, can be used in decorative grouping on large, low tables or chests, or upon the floor, and be combined with large branches of greenery and other plants.

The bazaar can be a gay market of booths decorated with Bible plants. Booths made of pine boughs, palm leaves, branches of myrtle and of other "goodly trees" may be reminders of those days of harvest celebration when the Israelites were commanded by God to dwell in booths and to rejoice in Him. The booth of olives could be decorated with fruitful boughs of olive, made of paper for the occasion, and with doves, made of paper pulp and poised on branches, while others could be in flight, each bearing a twig of olive in its beak.

A booth of bells, hung with paper bells and pomegranate foliage, flowers and fruit, will make a charming booth in which to sell needlework, jewelry, kitchen utensils or any object in which a bell design is used.

A booth in which even the men can take part in decorating is the one dedicated to the happy days when nations shall beat their swords into plowshares, and each citizen shall sit safe and unafraid under his vine and fig tree. Crossed swords or crossed guns could be hung on the wall immediately below a placard on which have been lettered the words of Micah (*4:3-4*). Other war trophies belonging to the men of the church could be used in the booth, and garden implements could be used also in dressing the booth, or even become items of sale.

When we consider the items for sale at the bazaar, the possibilities of Bible plant products are almost inexhaustible. Everything from canned, preserved, dried and candied fruits, grapejuice, olive oil and bread, to dairy products and honey, can be offered for sale. It was the plants of Palestine that made it a land flowing with milk and honey; cows were dependent upon green pastures, and the honey bees upon the flowers of the land.

Packages of Bible plant seeds might prove a popular item. These seeds may be harvested from the gardens of church members, or bought from a seed house and resold. Bulbs, depending upon the season, may also be sold to gardeners. If the time is right, pots of anemones and hyacinths, and bowls of white narcissi, just about to bloom, can be sold. Collections of dried Bible plant material, to be used in flower arrangements, could be made into attractive saleable items.

Dried herbs and spices, packed in pottery jars or other containers, or in cellophane packages, should be popular items of sale. Packages may be made interesting by a decorated label bearing the name of the contents, and a Bible quotation referring to it.

The flax and linen booth can take its color scheme from the blue of flax flowers and the white of linen. Everything from linen handkerchiefs to cup towels may be on sale in this booth, as well as other products made from flax.

An interest in plants of the Bible, as we have seen, may lead to new pleasures in both gardening and entertainment, but one of the most important uses we can make of such an interest is that of teaching the Bible to the young. The reality of Bible people and Bible times is oftentimes not appreciated by children or even teenage boys and girls, but the growing of Bible plants can do much to make the young Bible student realize that those times were as real as our own. Sunday School pupils of all ages can participate in building the church garden, doing everything from collecting stones for paths and pools, to contributing plants and shrubs and organizing planting ceremonies in connection with them. The Sunday School class as a whole might contribute a Cedar of Lebanon, purchased perhaps as a living Christmas tree, from the nurseryman. Bible plants can also be grown by the children in boxes or in flower pots, as a class project or in cooperation or in friendly rivalry between classes. Unless the project is an extensive one, it is important to choose plants that are easy to grow, in order that some result may be assured. An interesting project that could be worked on indoors is to build the church or home Bible garden in miniature—sand, pebbles, cork, paper, paint, glue, and a few tacks or pins should be equipment enough.

An easily managed Sunday School project is an exhibit of Bible plants used today, for which the children can bring specimens from home. Spices, dried figs, dates, lentils, bits of linen, ripe grapes, apricots, and other fruits, almonds, walnuts, pistachio nuts—a variety of exhibits will suggest themselves. And one advantage, certain to be appreciated by small children, is that many of the specimens can be eaten when the display is over.

A more elaborate project for older classes can develop from such an exhibit, if we assemble the oldest economic plants known to man, labeling the Bible plants, and then showing the current use and value of these products in American life. The plants could be represented by models made by various members of the Sunday School, or by drawings and even photographs. Guide strings could lead from each model or photograph to placards arranged in groups in the foreground. On the placards will appear the name of the plant and other information. Perfume plants, herbs and spices should be included in this exhibit as well as grains, fruits and vegetables.

Geographical factors can be studied also in connection with these economic plants of the Bible—the location of the various merchant cities which were centers for the trade in perfume and precious woods, and the route of the "corn ships" which carried rations for the Roman Army in New Testament times, and made the Mediterranean a highway for the spreading of the gospel.

Interest in Bible plants leads directly to an interest in the land itself, and to build a miniature land of Palestine with its mountains, plains and boundaries will be fascinating to children and grown-ups alike. On the west will be the Mediterranean, to the south and east the deserts, to the north the Lebanon Mountains with cedars and other evergreens. The river can cut its deep valley from north to south to a point way below sea level, emptying into the Dead Sea. In the valley above the Dead Sea there should be a long grove of palm trees, in which the city of Jericho, "the city of palm trees," should be built.

On the maritime plain there should also be palm trees, although great fields of grain will be the most prominent vegetation. The plain of Esdraelon in the North will have its grain fields, too. War chariots, horses and camel caravans may take their place on these plains, for here were the roads of both trade and war.

Olive trees may be scattered throughout the land, but especially in the southern part of Judah, where it was too dry for many other trees to grow. In these southern foothills were good pasture lands, however, so that sheep, goats and cattle should be shown grazing here. On the very top of one of the mountains of Judah can be built the walled city of Jerusalem, with its Temple. And throughout the land, terraced hillsides covered with grapevines should be built.

Springs and fountains can be represented as flowing

from hill and mountainside, and around them a dense and lush vegetation. Oases, pools and wells can be scattered through the land and small thorny twigs can be placed throughout the whole length and breadth of the country to represent the ever present thorn and thistle. As many or as few plants of the land can be included as interest the children, but the placing of vines, figs, olives, palms, grain fields and cedars will give the child an excellent idea of the land and its vegetation. Lions and eagles, locusts and scorpions can be among the animals represented. Doves should appear in the countryside and in the city, for pigeons in the city of Jerusalem must have been as typical as pigeons in the city of New York.

This project can be extended, of course, to take in all of the Eastern part of the world, which had its effect upon the life of the people of the Bible just as it has upon us today. Egypt and the Nile country have been a tremendous influence in civilization and were actually the scene of hundreds of years of Israelite life.

Most helpful of all, in linking the Bible promises to our own times, might be a "rainbow" project—a study of the cycle of water and plant life, and, the symbolic interpretation of natural laws. Such a study begins with God's promise to Noah, and man's recognition that land and water are indeed ruled by law rather than by chance. Next should come consideration of the physical cycle of rainfall, with its relation to agriculture and the welfare of mankind. Finally, man's own part in maintaining or restoring the balance of nature can be studied, with special reference to the reclamation work being done in modern Palestine and in various parts of the United

States. If this study is to be in detail, information of value can be obtained from government bulletins; and maps and models may be made to illustrate current problems of trees and watersheds, soil conservation and land use.

Sunday School classes in which such lessons are learned may well prove an inspiration to the whole church community; for children, like plants, grow toward the light. And they will have no difficulty in entering into the spirit of the Bible teaching, by way of the study of plants. There must be healthy growth in any church community in which children, as well as elders, can lay hold of the lovely promise of the rainbow:

"While the earth remaineth, seedtime and harvest, and cold and heat, and summer and winter, and day and night shall not cease."

Arrangement by Constance Spry, Inc.

An easily accomplished arrangement for home or church which includes wheat, poplar, trembling aspen, box, savin juniper, sweet bay and sycamore.

Index